D1247983

THE DUSUN

A NORTH BORNEO SOCIETY

BY

THOMAS RHYS WILLIAMS

CASE STUDIES IN
CULTURAL ANTHROPOLOGY

GENERAL EDITORS

George and Louise Spindler

STANFORD UNIVERSITY

THE DUSUN

A North Borneo Society

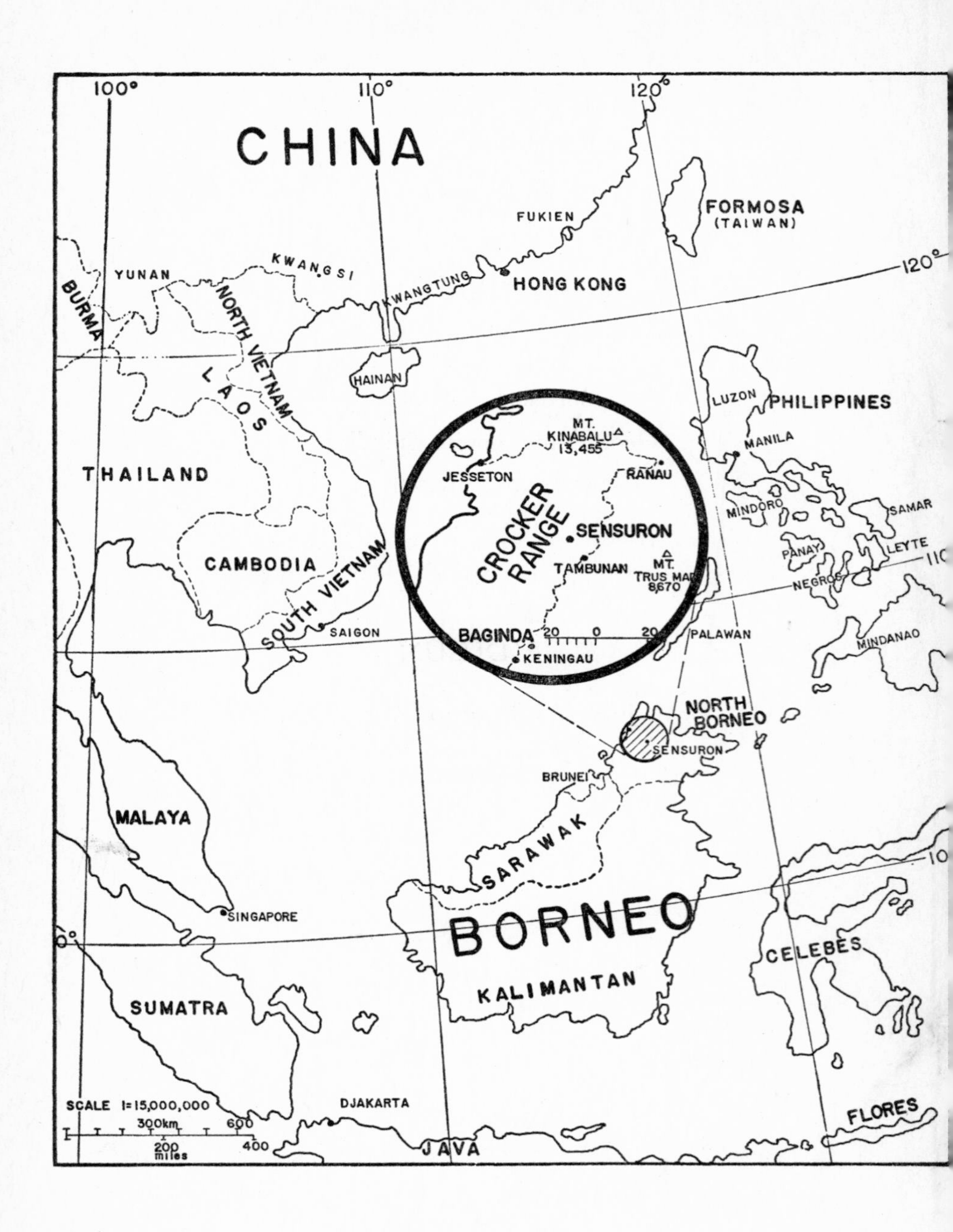

100°
110°
120°
CHINA
FUKIEN
FORMOSA
(TAIWAN)
KWANGSI
YUNAN
KWANGTUNG
HONG KONG
BURMA
NORTH VIETNAM
HAINAN
LAOS
LUZON
PHILIPPINES
MANILA
MT.
KINABALU
13,455
JESSETON
RANAU
THAILAND
CROCKER
RANGE
SENSURON
MINDORO
SAMAR
CAMBODIA
TAMBUNAN
MT.
TRUS MADI
8,670
PANAY
LEYTE
NEGROS
SOUTH VIETNAM
SAIGON
BAGINDA
20
0
20
PALAWAN
MINDANAO
KENINGAU
NORTH
BORNEO
SENSURON
BRUNEI
MALAYA
SARAWAK
SINGAPORE
BORNEO
CELEBES
KALIMANTAN
SUMATRA
SCALE 1=15,000,000
300km
600
200
miles
400
DJAKARTA
JAVA
FLORES

THE DUSUN

A North Borneo Society

By

THOMAS RHYS WILLIAMS

Ohio State University

HOLT, RINEHART AND WINSTON

NEW YORK CHICAGO SAN FRANCISCO TORONTO LONDON

Illustration on cover is of female specialists in ritual seeking to divine the nature of the sickness of a dying man.

March, 1966

Library of Congress Catalogue Card Number: 65–17659
29430–0115
Printed in the United States of America

Foreword

About the Series

These case studies in cultural anthropology are designed to bring to students in the social sciences insights into the richness and complexity of human life as it is lived in different ways and in different places. They are written by men and women who have lived in the societies they write about, and who are professionally trained as observers and interpreters of human behavior. The authors are also teachers, and in writing their books they have kept the students who will read them foremost in their minds. It is our belief that when an understanding of ways of life very different from one's own is gained, abstractions and generalizations about social structure, cultural values, subsistence techniques, and other universal categories of human social behavior become meaningful.

About the Author

Thomas Rhys Williams is a professor of anthropology at Ohio State University, Columbus, Ohio. He holds a doctoral degree in anthropology from Syracuse University and a master of arts degree in anthropology from the University of Arizona, Tucson. He has engaged in field research among the Papago of Arizona and native peoples of Borneo. His interests in field research include socialization, social structure, nonverbal communication, and cultural structuring of perceptions, including touch, color, and sight. He has published a variety of works in a range of professional journals, including those cited here, and presently is completing a text on Dusun socialization. He is a Fellow of the American Anthropological Association, a member of the Society of Sigma Xi, and other professional associations.

About the Book

The reader will discover that Thomas Williams takes him into a strange and unfamiliar world—that of the Dusun of Sensuron village in North Borneo. Dusun life is not simple. The many rituals, the Dusun concepts of life and death, of health and disease, of fortune and misfortune, and the patterns of subsistence, kinship and social organization, and of authority and justice make this way of life complex and compelling. This case study is unusual not only because the Dusun are unusal but because the author has managed to give us the details of the way of life in a compact volume without losing the reader in a maze of unrelated ethnographic facts. It is clear that Dr. Williams knows the Dusun intimately and that he grasps the main elements of Dusun life which give this culture coherence and meaning. Fortunately this culture has retained its character, and the author has been able to experience it as an intact, vital way of life. But the winds of change are blowing, even in remote Sensuron, and Dr. Williams gives us, in his final statements, a sense of the transforming scene to which the Dusun must adjust.

George and Louise Spindler
General Editors

Stanford, California
August 1965

Preface

I WENT to North Borneo in 1959 to begin systematic study of customary behavior of the Dusun, a native Borneo society. I was assisted by my wife in the research. My work in Borneo was supported by research grants from the National Science Foundation (G–5018; G–22110) and the Joint Committee on Asian Studies, American Council of Learned Societies-Social Science Research Council (1959, 1962), and conducted with assistance from Eli Lilly Company and Abbott Laboratories.

We lived from August 1959 to August 1960 in Sensuron, a Dusun village in the central mountain area of North Borneo. The study in Sensuron was devoted specifically to gathering data concerning ways Dusun teach their children customary behavior.[1] In 1962, under new grants of funds from sources supporting our 1959–1960 research, and with our 13-month-old son, we returned to continue study in another Dusun village in North Borneo. Our one year of residence in Baginda village, near Keningau, some 70 miles south of Sensuron, was concerned with determination of the validity and reliability of data gathered in Sensuron and more detailed inquiries about areas of customary behavior we had been unable to study in our first year of work. I was fortunate in having the capable assistance of Mr. Anthony Gibon in the course of most of my work in Sensuron and wish to express my gratitude to him.

We wish to express our gratitude also to these persons for their assistance in our study in Sensuron: Fathers Putman, Connelly, and Daporz of the Tobu and Tambunan Mill Hill Catholic missions, and John and Brenda Fryer of the Lands and Survey Department. We learned much from our friends *O. K. K.* G. S. Sundang, and Arusap, the late Tulid Murut native chief. Mr. Stephen Awong, our assistant in Baginda, was of invaluable help in our work and a friend of worth. We have benefitted greatly from the advice of Margaret Mead and are appreciative of her time and help in our work. My colleague Robert Theodoratus assisted me in citations to Southeast Asian peoples. William G. Solheim II provided a detailed critique on materials in Chapter 1. I very much appreciate the help of a number of my senior colleagues in my work and want to particularly thank Douglas Haring, E. H. Spicer, Fred Eggan, and Sherwood L. Washburn. I owe special thanks to my wife, Peggy, for her help under difficult conditions

[1] The term "customary behavior" refers to human behavior that is *learned, shared* widely in a society, *patterned* in its occurrence, and is *transmitted* from one generation to the next by means of symbolic communication, both in language and act. Not all human behavior is customary. Thus, some behavior forms are learned and shared with others in a social group, and often patterned in expression, but are not transmitted regularly to succeeding generations.

of fieldwork. Finally, I should like to say that we have had memorable personal experiences among the Dusun people, which demonstrate that men can learn to transcend the barriers of race, language, and culture. We are grateful to our Dusun friends for their patience and sympathy in our efforts to learn of their ways.

THOMAS RHYS WILLIAMS

August 1965

Contents

A Dusun mother preparing a harvest mat in her home.

Ilos, a Dusun headman, and his three-year-old son.

An eight-year-old girl plays at husking rice.

A Sensuron mother preparing a wet-rice field for planting.

A male specialist engaged in ritual to protect the community from epidemic disease.

Sensuron at midday of harvest, 1960. Author's residence is second on the left.

1

The Background of Dusun Customary Behavior

Geography

BORNEO IS the world's third largest island. Only Greenland and New Guinea are larger. The 293,000 square mile island lies across the equator between 4 degrees south and 8 degrees north latitudes and extends from east longitudes 108 to 119 degrees. To the north of Borneo, across the Sulu Sea, are the Philippine Islands. On the east, across the Strait of Macassar, are the islands of the Celebes. On the south, across the Java Sea, are the islands of Java and Bali, while to the west, where the Java and South China seas meet, is the island of Sumatra and the Malay Peninsula. To the northwest of Borneo, across the China Sea, are the mainland Southeast Asia areas of Vietnam and Cambodia.

Borneo is sparsely populated. An estimated 3,500,000 people live on the island, for an average density of population of about 12 persons to each square mile.

The island now is divided into three political units. Indonesian Borneo, or *Kalimantan,* contains 70 percent of the island land area and 70 percent of the population. A second political unit, with 79,000 square miles and 976,000 persons, is comprised of the two new Malaysia states of Sarawak and Sabah (North Borneo). The third political unit of 2000 square miles and 55,000 persons is Brunei, a state existing through agreement as a protectorate of the British government.

Seventy-five percent of Borneo vegetation is primary forest. The remainder of the land is covered with coastal and swamp vegetation or with secondary forest regrown in areas of shifting cultivation of crops. The forests spread over a complex of mountain ranges. A central range runs across the island along a northeast-southwest axis at elevations of 5000–6000 feet. Two other ranges, of the same general elevation, spiral out in an east-west direction from the middle of the central range, running generally to the coast areas as long descending ridges. Along the west and north coast there are large areas of hills, with several regions of narrow coastal plains and low swampy places associated with mouths of large rivers. In the south and east regions of the island there are large low areas of forest broken by intermittent hills and one short mountain range rising to 5000 feet. There are many low lakes in the eastern and southern areas of the island.

Borneo topography is dominated by Mt. Kinabalu, rising to 13,455 feet at the north end of the central mountain range. The highest peak in Southeast Asia, Kinabulu is exceeded in elevation only by the mountains of New Guinea and peaks of the Himalayas.

Borneo forests are divided into five zones, depending on elevation of the land. Above 6500 feet there are typical mountain grasses and shrubs. Between 4000 and 6500 feet are found stunted vegetation, often covered in dense, clinging festoons of moss. Between 2000 and 4000 feet there are oaks and chestnuts, with some conifers. The great tropical rain forest vegetation is found in the coastal lowlands and ranges below 2000 feet. Here thick trees rise more than 100 feet to a dense, leafy canopy intertwined above the forest floor. So little sunlight penetrates the forest canopy that only scattered shrubs and grasses survive. There is little color, except for the occasional splash of hues of an orchid, and only the sounds of a distant bird call breaks the silence. Along the coastal area vegetation is mostly herbs, grasses, and low shrubs. In some river mouth areas there are dense regions of mangrove swamps.

The eight major rivers of Borneo rise in the high reaches of the interior mountains and run their broad courses in a tumbling rush to the sea. Bornean rivers are vital as main routes of communication and trade because of the great difficulty of foot travel over the interior mountain ranges.

All of Borneo lies in the tropical climate zone and outside of the Asian and Pacific typhoon wind belt. The climate is marked by high temperatures and humidity and between 100 and 200 inches of annual rainfall. The yearly cycle of Borneo climate is divided into two monsoon phases. In the period from October through March of each year the prevailing winds are from the northeast, while in the months from May through September, the winds blow from a southwest direction. In these two periods sudden, violent rains with heavy winds are typical. Dry spells occur for periods of up to three weeks at the times of changes of monsoon wind directions. During these times clear skies and strong sun cause great damage to forests and crops. Most rainfall runs off rapidly due to the character of Borneo soil, causing some rivers to rise more than 50 feet in a few hours. Prolonged rain causes heavy damage to land through severe flooding. Monsoon rains do not fall evenly on the island due to mountain ranges acting as barriers to lower level air-mass movement.

Average Borneo temperatures vary only four to five degrees over the course of a year. Along the coasts the temperature averages 78 F during the rainy months of the monsoons and about 82 F in other months. In areas above 2000 feet temperatures average about 70 F in monsoon periods and about 75 F in other months. Borneo temperatures range from a midday high of 95 F along the coasts to mountain-area morning lows of 50–55 F. The average humidity of the island varies from 58 to 85 percent depending on elevation and location.

This hot, damp forest land is home to a very rich and diverse animal life.

Larger animals of the forest include the rhinoceros, orangutan, monkey, wild ox, pig, bear, deer, and wildcat. Lowland rivers and swamps have large crocodiles, while both coast and lowland forest areas are home for lizards, flying foxes, and large bats. More than 150 kinds of snakes are found on the island. In the forest canopy there are more than 500 kinds of birds, including eagles, parrots, swifts, and the Borneo hornbill. On the forest floor are the constant companions of the traveler: several kinds of leeches and yet uncounted types of scorpions, spiders, ants, beetles, and crawling and flying insects. The fresh waters and coastal seas of the island teem with marine life as diverse and abundant as land life. Since there are no large carnivorous animals on the island, major dangers to human life are from poisonous snakes, spiders, scorpions, crocodiles, and stinging insects.

Human Biology

At various times in the glacial eras of prehistory many islands off Asia, including Borneo, formed part of the mainland. Human beings probably have lived in Borneo since the time of Homo pithecanthropus, at least a quarter million years ago. While no specific evidence of pithecanthropoids have been found on the island, due to geographic and local political restrictions on such searches, it appears likely that the earliest inhabitants of the land belonged to this group because of the numbers of such forms found in nearby Java and China, and because of the relative ease of movement across lands now submerged beneath the China Sea. The first modern human population in Southeast Asia, and the first to come to Borneo, probably was of a type often called "Negrito." Some peoples somewhat like this type now live in the isolated mountain interior of the island.

About 15,000 to 20,000 years ago there was a series of movements of a population, sometimes called Indonesian, sometimes Malayan, out from South China into Southeast Asia and the offshore islands. It appears that most of the present Borneo native population is derived from several Indo-Malayan migrations to the island. Individuals of this physical type often have wavy or straight hair, with deep nose roots and broad nose tips. Men often have brow ridges and women commonly have well-developed breasts. Skin color varies from yellow to dark brown, eyes are dark brown, and there is little face or body hair. A very slight inner eye fold and short stature, with thick chested bodies, are common among members of this group. Blood-group studies show the Borneo Indo-Malayan peoples to be marked by a particular blood type.[1]

People of the Negrito physical type are very short in stature, often under

[1] In terms used to describe blood-group gene types, Borneo Indo-Malayan peoples are typified by a higher frequency of gene I^B at the ABO locus, a higher frequency of gene L^M than L^N, and a total lack of the Kell positive factor and the I^{A2} allele. At the Rh gene locus there is a high frequency of R^1 and a reported absence of the r gene (Hulse, 1963, 266–431). The precise classification of blood-group factors provide a means of comparing the biology of different peoples to determine if they show any similarity in the frequency of particular blood-group elements. Since blood-group factors are based on gene types and are not easily influenced by diet, climate, or customary practices, they are useful in seeking to determine what relationships, if any, exist between peoples.

five feet, while their skin and eye colors are very much darker than those of Indo-Malayans. Negrito hair is also wooly rather than wavy or straight. The adult male Negrito often has abudant body and some face hair, while both men and women frequently have bulbous foreheads and very broad, flat nose tips. It was mistakenly supposed in the past that Southeast Asian Negrito groups were related to Negroes of Africa. Available information of blood-group gene frequencies shows the Negrito population to have no significant diffierences from Indo-Malayan blood-group gene frequencies, while there are no similarities of blood-group gene frequencies between African Negro populations and Southeast Asian Negritos. The blood-group gene similarity between the Negrito and Indo-Malayan populations, with their markedly different appearance in body and face features, would indicate (when considered with available prehistorical evidence) that the Indo-Malayan peoples probably became adapted physically to life in the tropic rain forests of Borneo through long-term intermixture with earlier Negrito populations, who long since were adjusted to rigors of such life (Hulse 1963: 355).

History and Culture Change

It has been noted that because local geographic and political factors have prevented needed studies, the occupation of Borneo by Homo pithecanthropus remains to be documented. However, it is possible to assume that Borneo was the home of early man. These men, from evidence in their sites in China and Java, made chopping tools from stone material such as quartz and chert, and lived mostly through hunting large and small animals.

The earliest human population in Borneo was succeeded about 50,000 years ago by the Negrito, a structurally modern human type. From archeological evidences now available it would appear most of Southeast Asia was bypassed by the advanced techniques of making stone tools that appeared between 20,000 and 30,000 years ago in Europe and West Asia. The Negrito group probably hunted game and followed a style of life little different from their pithecanthropoid predecessors. There is no evidence at present whether the Negrito population intermarried with the pithecanthropoid group after arriving in Borneo, or hunted them for food. It is likely the Negrito population was better able to reason than the pithecanthropoids and so could compete and survive in any conflicts for territory and game. It is also a possibility that the Negrito and pithecanthropoid groups could have lived in different areas of Borneo and had little contact with one another.

Sometime about 5000 or more years ago, somewhere in the tropical zone of Southeast Asia, agriculture based on cultivation of rice was developed. Growing of food, rather than hunting it, brought profound changes in the way of life of people adopting the new technique of subsistence. However, the change from a predominantly hunting life to an agricultural way of existence took place slowly in Southeast Asia. A general term *Hoabinhian,* after the name of an archeological site in Northern Vietnam, can be used to designate the practice of mixed hunting and agricultural custom that lasted from about 12,000 to 10,000 years before the present to some 2000 years ago over much of Southeast Asia.[2] Typical tools of Hoabinhian culture were heavy hand adzes flaked from stone pebbles, and grinding and pounding stones. Probably, the adze tool was used in clearing wild vegetation, while grinding and pounding stones were used in preparation of plant foods. Hoabinhians were fond of living in entrances to caves and rock shelters, and of supplementing their crop foods through collecting molluscs and hunting deer, pig, and wild oxen. It is probable this population represents the earliest of a series of at least four Indo-Malayan migrations to Borneo from the Asian mainland, although Hoabinhian remains have yet to be identified definitely from the archeological sites in Borneo systematically excavated by trained scholars.[3]

The three later migrations of Indo-Malayan populations to Borneo took place at different times, beginning about 2500 to 2000 B.C. These peoples were dependent for their living on raising of food, rather than hunting or mixed hunting and agricultural activities. The evidences of these three migrations are based on whether stone adzes were made in a lozenge or quadrangular cross section, refinements of adze shape, and on the use of pottery.

The earliest migration of a food-raising Indo-Malayan population to Borneo came with movement from South China and North Vietnam, through Formosa and the Philippines, of a people whose typical tool was a stone adze made in a lozenge cross section. Following this time, probably between 1500 to 1000 B.C., two closely related populations of Indo-Malayan food raisers, both using a quadrangular-sectioned adze, moved into Borneo from opposite directions; a first migration spread across the mainland of Southeast Asia into northeast India and down the Malay Peninsula into Sumatra, Java, and south Borneo, apparently replacing any Hoabinhian peoples that were there. At about the same time or slightly later, a second migration of quadrangular-sectioned adze makers moved out from South China and North Vietnam, through Formosa and the Philippines, to northern Borneo and the Celebes.

In both instances Indo-Malayan quadrangular adze makers depended for their living on growing dry rice and yams, and keeping domestic pigs. They made pottery by hand, often with the aid of a beater, which sometimes was wrapped with cord to give a textured finish to the outside of the pottery. The spread of all of these populations over a distance involving open seas probably means that the quadrangular and lozenge adze were boat building as well as agricultural tools.

So far as can be determined from recent linguistic evidences the Indo-Ma-

---

[2] There is no conclusive evidence at present of agricultural practices in sites typical of Hoabinhian culture. It is likely such evidences will be found. The term "Hoabinhian" is used here to avoid introduction of a new term or use of another term, in a literature which tends to be confusing and contradictory concerning this era of Southeast Asia culture history.

[3] It is held widely at present that the Hoabinhian population was ancestral to the modern Melanesian population and is not at all Indo-Malayan in type. This conclusion is far from certain and not supported by available physical evidences. It can be argued that Hoabinhian remains show Indo-Malayan phenotypic characteristics.

layan and Negrito populations of Borneo today speak dialects of the Malayo-Polynesian language stock. Except for languages of the natives of Australia and a small number of languages of Papuan New Guinea, all the languages of the Pacific islands belong to this same stock.

The earliest written records that appear to mention Borneo and its peoples are found in Indian documents. What seem to be references to Borneo appear in the *Ramayana,* a collecton of Indian sacred texts dating from the sixth to third centuries B.C.

Historic records appear to indicate that during the first five centuries, A.D. sea trade and travel developed between China and India, mainly due to the spread of Buddhism through China in the third and fourth centuries A.D. Buddhist scriptures were brought by sea to China by Indian missionaries, and Chinese converts sailed to India on pilgrimages. It is possible that these voyages could have been interrupted on the west coast of Borneo for rest and supplies, although there is at present no reliable evidence of any such events taking place. In the period from A.D. 500 to 1300 Chinese and Indian traders could have stopped along the west and south coasts of Borneo. By the twelfth century A.D. a political unit on the west coast of the island, called *Burune* in Javanese records, was noted in Chinese documents as paying subject tribute to the Chinese emperor. In the twelfth and thirteenth centuries A.D. Indian cultural influences were brought to south Borneo by agents of the Sumatra-based Hindu empire of *Sri Vijaya.* In the late thirteenth century A.D. the Java Hindu empire of *Majapahit* replaced *Sri Vijaya's* political control in Borneo. Records of the early Chinese Ming Dynasty (A.D. 1370–1430) note what appears to be contacts with trade colonies of Chinese in Borneo, although there is question of the accuracy of these accounts. After the overthrow of the Mongol forces by Ming armies in A.D. 1368, a series of large naval forces were reported to have sailed into the China Sea area to extract tribute and homage to the new empire. Borneo may have been visited by several of these missions.

About this time Indian and Arab traders began regular visits to Borneo, using as a base the port of Malacca on the Malay Peninsula. On these visits Arab traders and their Malaccan Malay Moslem converts spread the Islamic tradition to Borneo coastal peoples. By the late fifteenh century A.D. Chinese records note reports of a strong native Moslem state in the area of Brunei Bay paying tribute to the Moslem sultan of Malacca. Elsewhere in Borneo Moslem ideas were spread to south and east coast populations by Moslemized Javanese and Sumatran traders and officials. By the time of the first European contacts with Borneo in A.D. 1521 Brunei was a town of 25,000 Moslems, controlling most of the west, north, and east coast areas of the island, as well as the southern islands of the Philippines.

Between the first visit of Portuguese to Brunei in 1521 and the late nineteenth century British colonization of North Borneo, Portuguese, Spanish, Dutch, and English were attracted to Borneo by accounts of vast riches in gold and diamonds and through a desire to obtain control of the spice market for European commerce. In the sixteenth and seventeenth centuries European contacts with Borneo peoples were sporadic, short-term trade efforts. The main areas of competition between European colonial forces generally were outside of Borneo until the close of the eighteenth century. At the beginning of the latter century Southeast Asia, including Borneo, had been exposed to direct contact with Europeans for nearly 200 years. Yet this long period of contact appears to have altered local custom very little, since the pattern of trade by each European nation was to attempt to control the seas with naval forces, then to capture key seaports and to build forts to protect warehouses in which trade goods were gathered. Few Europeans of this period learned local languages or lived outside of fort areas. Thus, social contacts were minimal between Europeans and native people. However, in the eighteenth century the Dutch altered this pattern of contact by taking control of local government affairs in Java and Sumatra in order to prevent local wars from interrupting trade. This means of contact with the local population became the European pattern of Southeast Asian colonialism in the next 200 years. In this time, as European nations captured seaports and built forts in new areas, their forces moved inland to take control of local affairs, according to their own customary views of the ways native matters should be conducted.

During the eighteenth and nineteenth centuries the Dutch and English contended for political control of Borneo. As these powers moved into the ports along the coasts of the island they found a dual local culture. Around the coasts there were small populations derived from other areas—Javanese along the south and east coasts, Malays along the west and north coasts, with Chinese mixed in among both populations. In the interior, living behind coastal hills and mountains, were the Indo-Malayan native populations. In most Borneo seaports Javanese and Malays became minor officials for the Dutch and English, while Chinese took over most trade activities. Colonial control of Borneo has been extended and maintained generally through use of these nonnative populations.

At the beginning of the nineteenth century Dutch control over south and east Borneo had been extended to all key ports and some parts of the nearby inland areas. The English made two unsuccessful attempts to colonize the island in the eighteenth century, but were driven out by native forces. It was not until after the 1840s that English attempts at Borneo colonization were successful, through efforts of various individuals seeking personal fortunes. In such instances the British government gave military support for control of Borneo areas by its private citizens.

In the nineteenth century activities of Dutch and English colonial forces in Borneo generally were confined to keeping control of coastal areas. Interior areas remained largely unknown because of fears of attacks by natives and due to difficulties of travel. It was not until the second decade of the twentieth century that colonial forces became apparent in interior areas of the island. Today there are regions of the center of the island which have yet to be visited by Europeans and for which no accurate maps exist.

The Setting of the Study

The village of Sensuron is located in the northern end of the Borneo central mountain range at an elevation of 2300 feet. The community, comprised of 947 members of Dusun society, is situated above the northwestern edge of the 3 by 10 mile Tambunan plain, some 70 miles south of the heights of Mt. Kinabalu. The plain contains 10,000 Dusun in 36 communities, ranging in population from 75 to 250 persons. Sensuron is the largest village in the area and the largest native community in North Borneo. The village, with 183 house structures, stretches over a quarter by one mile area on top of a 50-foot high river bluff south of the Sensuron River. Sensuron is the oldest community on the Tambunan plain, and it is the point from which some 19 other Tambunan villages were settled. The people of Sensuron are descendents of at least four villages that moved in the 1850–1890 period from the nearby high mountain elevations to begin to clear the Tambunan plain land for irrigated rice agriculture.

Today lower hill slopes about the village generally are cleared for gardens of yams, tapioca, squash, corn, and a variety of vegetables. Higher elevations about the village and most land beyond a five mile radius of the Tambunan plain are covered by primary forest. Here plant and animal life is abundant and provides a substantial supplement to the village diet. To the east of the Tambunan plain the forests about the peak of Mt. Trus Madi, rising to 8670 feet, provide plentiful vegetation and game.

The climate of the Tambunan area is subject to the two annual monsoon cycles, with a moderate annual rainfall averaging some 73 inches. Temperatures in Sensuron range from highs of 92 F to lows of 54 F with a relative humidity ranging between 54 and 69 percent.

The people of Sensuron are predominately Indo-Malayan in physical appearance, with some five percent of the villagers showing some Negrito characters. The two dialects spoken in the community are Malayo-Polynesian. There are some loan words from all cultural contact languages used in the village, and the general style of life reflects some borrowing of forms of custom over centuries of indirect influences from outside cultures. In general the cultural level of Sensuron village is well beyond that of the Borneo forest nomads of the central mountain jungles. Yet the style of Sensuron life is not that of Dusun along the west North Borneo coastal plain, where direct contacts with other cultures continually have occurred over the past 700 years or more. Changes are taking place rapidly in Sensuron as a result of control by English colonial police and administrative officers, the Japanese army occupation of Tambunan in 1942–1945, and since the political independence of North Borneo in 1963 as a state of the new nation of Malaysia.

Physically, linguistically, and culturally the 145,000 Dusun of North Borneo have more in common with a number of native groups in the Philippines and Formosa than with native peoples in nearby Sarawak and Kalimantan. Available evidence tends to support the hypothesis that the Dusun of Sensuron are representatives of the Indo-Malayan quadrangular adze-maker population migrating to Borneo from the north.

The general behavior patterns of Sensuron are similar in form to those of Indo-Malayan and other native people in Southeast and Island Asia who have remained at the edge of change brought by Indian, Chinese, Moslem, and European cultural influences. Studies of customary behavior that have been conducted in these societies provide reference for comparison with the ways of the people of Sensuron. A brief bibliography has been included at the end of the text to provide a means of proceeding with comparative readings.

2

Conceptions of the Natural World

FOR THE DUSUN of Sensuron the natural universe is comprised of distinct aspects, clearly identified and controlled by forces and beings well known in form and habits. The universe is perceived as a giant coconut shell. The surface of the earth is seen as the collapsed, flattened dome of a more ancient coconut shell, which gave way infinitely before the creation of man, animals, and plants. The limits of the universe are expressed in the phrase *nEpEsu tAuAn,* literally, "a hole in the sky through which the unknown can be seen."[1]

The plane formed by the collapsed coconut dome is known as the place of Dusun daily activities and concerns. This surface is known to have edges, for in legend and folktale there are accounts of the movement of the sun, moon, and stars, "passing to the edge of the earth," or, "movement under the edge of the earth."

In the area above the plane of the earth, under the dome of the coconut shell, are natural phenomena called *gesAmuenAgEn,* "all things that exist above the earth." Stars are attached to the interior underside of the coconut dome. Stars that fall from place are known as *tie rambetEn,* or "star feces." Except for Venus, the Pleiades, and a cluster of stars about Beta Andromodae, stars and star groups are generally of little concern to Dusun. The Pleiades and the stars about Beta Andromodae, known to move in a fixed cycle, are used to determine specific times for burning of felled jungle and for planting crops in the yearly cycle of subsistence activities. Moving in a full circle, from under the edge of the earth at the direction of *koliun* ("where the sun peers out"), these star groups proceed up across the under-dome of the coconut shell and then down to the edge of the earth, known as *katAnAbEn* ("where the sun disappears").

The sun and moon are considered to have particular life histories. *SAdek-An,* of Sensuron, gave this account,

The sun is a man, while the moon is a woman. They are husband and

[1] For description of Tambunan Dusun vocoids and nonvocoids see T. R. Williams, "Tambunan Dusun Social Structure," *Sociologus,* Vol. 12, No. 2 (1962), p. 156.

wife. They do much of their work apart now, like people do, although it was not always that way. Once, the moon was also a sun too, and followed her husband just behind in his work. But, one day the great hunter *Saro* came to the edge of the earth and shot the second sun with his blowpipe, since any woman who had seen the second sun and was pregnant would lose the baby. The second sun died, and now is seen all pale at night, the wife of the sun who works in the day. Some days the moon and sun are seen in the sky together, as she tries to catch up to her husband. But she cannot, for he is forever *sinAdu peAlAtAn* ("one sky measure apart") from her because *Saro* killed her then.

Creation and the Creator

When asked by a child about the creation, or origin of the universe, a Dusun parent often responds with the comment, "this was made by the creator." From often repeated legends Dusun learn that man is a special creation of a specific act of *menemANEn* and *sumInEndu,* the male and female creator beings. The physical universe is known to be a creation of these beings. The creator pair are said to reside beyond the limits of the universe—in a duplicate of the human world that is infinitely better where food is more abundant; where there are no diseases, accidents, loss of property; and where there are no arguments, fights, or wars. When asked to describe the nature of the existence of the creator beings, Dusun usually reply that humans cannot experience that world directly, or even after death, since on their death men go to a world located somewhere near the top of Nabalu (*i.e.,* Mt. Kinabalu). There are widely known folktales that give details of creation and that are told by older persons at times of ritual feasting with family and close friends. *SAdekAn* of Sensuron recounted this tale.

There is a brother, *menemANEn*, and a sister, *sumInEndu.* These two are married. Together they created all that exists in this world. When they had finished they asked each other, "What are we to do with this earth?" So they decided to make a sky, but when they were done, it was too small to fit over all the edges of the earth. Too, the earth was very flat, with no hills and mountains. So, one of them got on each edge of the earth and pushed it hard into the middle to make it smaller, and so fit under the sky they had made before. In this way the creator pair made the hills and mountains you see today. Then *menemANEn* and *sumInEndu* looked about and said, "We will make man, and so from their intercourse they made the first men, from stone. They could not be hurt, and were very brave in war. They did not get sick, and did not eat much. But they could not speak, so they could not talk to work together, or ask for help of the creators. So *menemANEn* turned these men to rest and you can see them today in the jungle where they stand watching wisely over our affairs. These men stand guard in the villages today too. These people were replaced by men of wood, and they were also healthy, wise, and very strong, for being of wood they could not be cut by a knife. But the creator pair soon found they had no firewood, for they had used all the wood to make man. So they made these men into the great trees of the jungle, especially the *sEgIndi* and *nunuk* trees you see today, where they stand to help man when he needs aid. Then the creators had intercourse and made men of clay (earth) and they were like the men now, for some were strong, others weak, some well, some always ill. When these people died, they went back to earth, like we do now. But the creators were not happy with these men of earth because they could grow no food without earth, so they took these men and put them over the surface of the world, where they now help us grow our food and feed our animals. Then the creators had intercourse and made two beings, a brother called *kAki kAki* and a sister called *kEdukEdu*. These beings were not people like us, but were *Asundu* ("sacred") and very wise. They had intercourse and a first child, a male named *kudINkIN,* and then a female child named *tINAleg.* These two were brother and sister. Then there was a third child, a male called *kEmpetAs,* and a fourth child, a female named *sANerAn.* These two were also brother and sister. Then *kudINkIN* and *tINAleg* had intercourse and from this came all the Dusun people of today. And *kEmpetAs* and *sANerAn* had intercourse and from this came all the spirits and disease givers we know today.

In a general sense Dusun view their relationships with the creators as one of stability and fairness. Men do not exist in relation to a creator who is felt to be wrathful and awesome, although merciful, as in the early Judaic conception of God. Nor do Dusun see the creator beings as mysterious and unknowable, perpetrators of injustices and disasters beyond all proportion to the actual guilt of man, as in the tradition of the Greeks in the fifth century B.C. To Dusun the creators are all powerful, all pervasive, and the focal point of all known being. Creator beings are felt not to directly intercede in human affairs unless specifically requested by a male ritual specialist; such requests usually are made only with reference to community crises of famine, flood, drought, or disease. Personal crises, which are caused by supernatural beings of lesser influence in the universe, such as the children of *kEmpetAs* and *sANerAn,* are the concern of and within the usual scope of control of female ritual specialists.

Time[2]

In one aspect time is conceived by Dusun as a result of the movement of the sun, moon, and particular stars about a circle inscribed on the inner side of the coconut shell universe. Each full cycle of the sun around the plane of the earth is termed as *tAdau,* or day, and is divided into specific segments. Cycles of days are multiplied into larger units of seasons, and seasons are added to create the time segment of a year. The portion of time corresponding to the Western concept of month is determined through appearance of the moon. The concept of

---

[2] The interpretation of time concepts here follows the ideas of E. R. Leach. See *Rethinking Anthropology,* London, London School of Economics Monographs on Social Anthropology, No. 22, Athlone Press, 1961.

a month is used to determine specific times of labor and leisure and is not expanded usually to comprise larger units of time.

In a second aspect time is conceived as a point along a line beginning "at the start of the world," or creation, and running on to a point in the distant future known as *tAhune,* or "afterwards," a time when "all sickness will vanish, men will be reborn to live forever, and there will be no hunger and war." Along this finite line, which is supposed to cross under, and at a right angle to the *Koliun-katAnAbEn* cycle, time proceeds from an immediate present, determined from the place of the sun, moon, or stars in the sky overhead, a point termed *biAnE* ("now"), to a future time close at hand, *tAure* ("just later"), from a past close at hand, *dE tenE* ("just past").

In the first instance described here, the idea of time is a category of Dusun experience in which certain phenomena regularly repeat themselves. From recurrence of cycles of the sun, moon, and particular stars Dusun have constructed a series of intervals in experience that are compounded to provide reference points for social behavior. Days are multiplied to seasons, seasons to calendar rounds, and calendar rounds to ritual cycles and multiples of ritual cycles, lasting beyond the life of any one individual. In the second instance described, time is expressed as a category of Dusun experience in which there is an irreversible process of an inexorable nature. When a Dusun marks his place on the line of time from the "creation" to the "afterwards," he conceives it marked finally, as a point on his steady progression along that line.

Time is conceived also in Dusun experience to be a pendulumlike oscillation between opposites. Between day and night, life and death, feast and famine, wet and dry seasons, and numerous other pairs of contraries in Dusun existence there is held to be an entity that swings back and forth between opposite objects or events. The life force of a man is at one instant in a living body and the next in a grave, while there is between plenty and starvation a fate (*lEmAg*) that cojoins these opposites. The creation is viewed as the point of origin of all known opposites in Dusun life. Such contraries are inescapable, since each set exists without reference to the desires of men.

Time is conceived in a fourth aspect, that of similar pairs, or sets of pairs of persons linked by an event in "time." Between siblings of the same sex, as members of a "pair of children," there is the event of sharing the same *posud,* or umbilical cord. It is common for Dusun to speak of their older or younger brothers or sisters by use of the terms *irenadi* ("as I am"), *mipinai kito* ("born of the same parents"), or *topuposud* ("sharing the same umbilical cord"). The event cojoining the pair of kin is an event in time, conceived as neither a repetitive, nonrepetitive, nor an oscillation process. Rather, in this fourth conception, time is an act or occurrence that creates a bond of similarity of a durable nature. Such event-linked similar pairs, or sets of pairs, are an essential part of the fabric of Dusun social relationships. Too, opposites of kin linked in unlike pairs joined through existence of an event in time form another vital aspect of Dusun kinship relations. Dusun see father and son, or father-in-law and son-in-law as unlike pairs, kin joined by an event in time—birth, marriage, and so on.

Climate, Animals, and Plants

Winds are said to come from openings located at the far edges of the earth. The openings, "navels of the winds," are supposedly small, but passing through to the lower area of the universe. Adjacent to openings of the wind are similar apertures from which rains are said to derive. These openings, "navels of the water," are felt to be the source of water in clouds and the place of origin of the sea. When heavy rain falls, Dusun say the clouds have become so burdened with water that they must sink to earth. Rivers and streams are seen as points of collection of water from fallen clouds. Clouds are formed also through collection of smoke from jungle burning and cooking fires. Fog and mist also are said to be "fallen" clouds. Drought is explained as the deliberate act of some offended supernatural blocking the navels of the waters. The infrequent high winds of the jungle highlands are said to be caused by angry supernaturals enlarging the navel of the wind to cause an increase in wind speed. A variety of ritual acts are employed to control or alleviate unusual conditions of rain, winds, or drought.

Lightning is explained as the sign of a spirit being that transports a corpse to beyond Mt. Kinabalu, while thunder is the sound of a body being taken from the ground. The duration of a thunder storm is taken as a measure of the intensity of struggle by spirits for possession of a body.

The appearance of a rainbow is considered to be a sign of a day of misfortune. When parents note a rainbow they call to their children to come home immediately, for the rainbow is known to be the path for a particular form of evil supernatural, or *pAmAEbiE,* in their descent to earth in search of human victims. A rainbow is said to always end in mud and muddy places, the favorite habitat of *pAmAEbiE.*

High and low sun temperatures are said to be products of the sun coming too close to earth, and of the obscuring of the sun by clouds, or due to the sun's absence at night. *Moshi* of Sensuron related this story of the origin of the sun's heat,

> There was a time when the days were always cold. So the creator said, "It is too hard to always be cutting wood to keep warm. I must warm the world without having to cut wood." So he took a brand burning in his firepit and pushed it together in his hands and then went outside and threw it up into the sky, where it went very far and fell into the sky known by men today. He threw that thing so hard that it still is moving about the sky now, from his strong arm. Sometimes the warmth from that sun is not so great because there is so much smoke from burning the jungle for planting. Then it is cold.

It is believed that because man was created especially by the creator beings, he is essentially of a different nature from all animals. Animals are said to have been created for human food. The creator beings brought plants to the world to allow animals to live. Some plants, used by man, were created only for his use, and are not eaten by animals. There are a variety of more than 30 folk-tales regarding creation of specific animals and plants. *Dao,* the headman of Sensuron village, told this story of the origin of the sago palm and the sago "beetle":

> There was a beautiful girl who was asleep in her house in the middle of the day. As the young hunter Saro passed that girl's house he heard her call out in her sleep, "cut me bamboo to make a *sEmputan* (musical instrument)." So he did that, and took the bamboo to the girl. But when she came onto the veranda of the house, and he gave her the bamboo, she would not take it, saying, "I did not ask you for that". But her vagina called out to Saro and said, "it was this girl's vagina that called out for the bamboo!" The girl was very ashamed of that, and ran into the house. Then, being very ashamed of her vagina, she went to the deep jungle and took it out and placed it on the stump of a tree. Then a deer came and rubbed its side against that vagina and left hair upon it. Then the tree stump grew again and became the sago palm and the vagina became the beetle you find inside there.

Matter, Sound, and Reflections

The term *kiempunAn,* or "stuff of the universe," designates the material that comprises any object. Beyond this definition there are no traditional explanations of the nature of matter. When the subject of the essence of natural objects is discussed, Dusun usually depend on the answer, *dau dau,* "it is natural". A question of "Why does water evaporate under heat?" receives the simple answer, *"dau dau."* Should a child, or an adult, persist in seeking an answer to the question of *nAkurA dau dau?* ("Why is that thing natural?"), he will be told, *earAd mAntAd d'iti* . . ., ("It has been like that from the creation.")

While talking with *SAdekAn* of Sensuron on the subject of the nature of matter, his seven-year-old great-grandson interrupted the conversation at his comment that matter had been the same since creation to ask, "Why has it been like that from the creation, grandfather?" Turning from me *SAdekAn* replied, "It is the will of the creator that it be so." Persisting, the boy asked, "Why has it been created by God in that manner?" Peering intently at the boy, *SAdekAn* quietly answered, "Go ask the creator!"

For Dusun there are several classifications of sound. A human shout reflected from a hillside is distinguished from the sound of a human voice in usual conversion. Objects are considered to have residual, or inherent, sounds, although any sound from an object must be caused by a man.

A human reflection in water or a mirror is known as the appearance of the departure of a soul of the individual (see Chapter 5). Although mirrors were in regular use in ten percent of Sensuron households, the greater number of Dusun in Sensuron still avoid their reflections in a mirror, since seeing the soul is a bad omen for health and life. In Sensuron, *Ousi,* a seventy-year-old woman, called the female ritual specialist to perform a special ceremony to recapture the soul seen escaping in her accidental glance in the mirror of a neighbor. Her death three weeks later was attributed by her sons to the glance in the mirror.

As recounted here Dusun ideas of natural events constitute one part of a larger framework for Dusun life. Other parts of that structure are described in chapters that follow. Together, these customary forms of belief and behavior make up a Dusun view of the world and of the meaning of human existence.

3

Religious Belief and Behavior

Belief in a Supernatural World

IN DUSUN LIFE there are a series of personal and community-wide crises that lead to fear of the unknown. The personal crises of birth, sickness, death, individual fortune, success in hunting, yield of crops, and outcome of personal disputes are marked by Dusun as events in which it is necessary to deal with the forces responsible through engaging in specific ritual behavior. Community crises of flood, drought, epidemic disease, and war similarly are dealt with through ritual behavior.

The people of Sensuron believe there is a direct relationship between the crises of life and a world of supernatural beings and unseen forces. It is also believed generally that proper ritual actions can be interposed between men and supernatural beings and forces in attempts to modify or control events causing fear, pain, or uncertainty.

The universe is known to be populated by several types of spirit beings and forces of good and harm. The differences between man and such beings and forces is believed the product of the special circumstances of creation of each group. In the origin and creation legend recounted in the previous chapter, the traditional account of differences between men and nonhuman forces and beings was described as deriving from intercourse of the creator beings *menemANEn* and *sumInEndu;* from this act there was produced the brother and sister *kAki kAki* and *kEdukEdu,* who from their intercourse produced four children, two males named *kudINkIN* and *kEmpetAs* and two females named *tINAleg* and *sANerAn.* In accounting for supernatural beings and forces of good and harm in the universe, *Dumbor,* a male ritual specialist, noted:

> There is a difference between men and those others in the world because of the way they were created. All men are the children of *kudINkIN* and his sister *tINAleg.* That marriage was good because it was the special way the creator made all of us. All the disease giver spirits are children of an incest marriage between *kEmpetAs* and his sister *sANerAn.* The marriage of *kudINkIN* and his sister was good, for although they were brother and sister, they paid the proper ritual fine (*sAgIt*) to cool off their offense

against the creator. Those other two did not pay the fine to cut their relationship and so all of their children are offspring of incest and have gone on having intercourse like animals. They live in an evil world, producing children without character or reason. Those disease givers are very jealous of man because of our favor with the creator. So they work to make us sick and to take away our luck, lure us to accidents in their rage at being forever evil and dirty.

At least 20 offspring of the incestuous union of *kEmpetAs* and *sANerAn* are named by Dusun as responsible for much human ill-fortune and the personal crises of life. Generally these beings are termed *tAmboreE,* or "disease givers." In addition, there are 20 other harmful supernatural beings, termed *rAgun,* or "souls of the dead," believed also responsible for the crises of life. Distinctions between disease givers and souls of the dead are clear in Dusun legend, folktale, and belief; disease givers are "owners" and guardians of animals of the jungle, water, air, trees, plants and fruits of the forest, soils of the fields, and rock of the mountains. Mostly human in appearance, disease givers are characterized as mischievous, capricious, and bent on making men appear as fools to the creator. In contrast, souls of the dead are known to be utterly foul in appearance, with disgusting human aspects and single-mindedly bent on capture and destruction of human souls. Disease givers are believed to have existed from creation times, while souls of the dead are felt to be human beings doomed by the creator at their death to an eternity of wandering and cannibalism because of evil deeds while alive.

In addition to members of these two groups of malevolent supernatural beings, there are three spirit beings known to have attributes of a beneficial nature. Most important of these in Dusun life is *bAmbariEn,* or "spirit of the rice." Known as guardian of the rice crop and storehouse, the rice spirit is supposed to be female in nature, in contrast to the male nature of all forms of disease givers and souls of the dead. The rice spirit has no specific story of origin, although it is agreed that the being has existed since the time of creation as the gift of the creator to man for insuring ample food.

The two other beneficial spirits, *mlnaret* and *sumAsaui,* are considered supernatural beings with humanlike attributes, whose concerns generally are to assist men in times of crises caused by disease givers and souls of the dead.

In addition to these five classes of supernatural beings, there is a special group of 25 spirit beings, whose attributes and powers are known and used by all female and some male ritual specialists. Termed "spirits of the *kAmbarANun,*" or "spirits of *kenEkeAn*", these beings are called upon by female ritual specialists as part of major divination, restoring and curing rituals, through use of supposed inherent powers of the root of the *kAmbarANun* plant ("sweet flag" or *Acornus calamus*), a cultivated marsh herb with a pungent rootstock odor. Generally held remote from everyday affairs, this group of supernatural beings can be reached and exercise their powers only in special acts involving the *kAmbarANun* plant.

Finally, there are believed to be at least five powers, or forces, abroad in the universe that affect the life of man. Three of the forces, termed *ausEN, tApun,* and *seseAn,* are supposed harmful, while the forces known as *Asundu* and *ApAgEn* are considered favorable to human concerns.

The power of *Asundu* commonly is said to refer to the curing powers of a female ritual specialist and the restorative abilities of the male ritual specialist, and is believed derived from the inexhaustible store of energy of the creator force, which is felt to be inherent in the universe.

It is a matter of great concern to Dusun that a person, object, or location possessed of considerable amounts of *Asundu* are to be treated with respect and generally avoided. Possession of an appreciable amount of this force creates the necessity for designation of *ApAgEn,* or "a walling off from human contacts." There is a fine for persons touching objects or entering locations termed *Ap-Agun.* Most often *ApagEn* forces residual in locations or objects are noted by a specially carved sign stick of wood or bamboo. This symbol serves notice of the existence of a condition of "sacredness." Such signs may be used on occasion also to mark personal property in the form of bamboo groves, stands of fruit trees, and garden lands.

When the three harmful forces are discussed, Dusun agree generally there is a clear distinction between each power. These distinctions are reflected in the comment of *Kumpiek,* a female ritual specialist:

> If a ritual specialist tries to harm a person with her powers, except for enemies in war, she would be struck down by the power of *ausEN* or *seseAn.* These are very bad powers, working alike, but different. She must be careful if she intends harm in her heart, for she will become sick and die from one of these powers. But *tApun* is the power that harms any person who refuses food or drink or a gift offered in friendship, or will come to a person who says they will do a thing for someone and then forgets. This power of *tApun* is from the creator, like *ausEN* and *seseAn,* and is all about us. The disease givers and souls of the dead dislike the smell of the *tApunAn* person and come to seek out the person who offends them.

Belief in the power of *tApun* is a most effective means of social control in Dusun life, particularly in the context of fears of poisoning, soul stealing, and personal disputes, since the idea tends to insure the participation of all persons at special gatherings for ritual and insures personal commitments will be hon-ored.

Ritual Specialists

It has been observed that Dusun fears of the unknown often involve use of a specialist in ritual behavior in attempts to divine the nature of illness, to undo unfortunate events, to restore matters to original conditions, to prevent sickness, or to provide protection against impending harm. Ritual specialists are important persons in a Dusun community. Both men and women may be specialists; the female specialist often is termed "a person knowing the rituals" while the male specialist usually is called "one who knows." Female specialists were most noticeable in the daily life of Sensuron, for there were seven women trained to undertake rituals. There were two male specialists in Sensuron in 1959–1960.

The social status of the male specialist generally is superior to that of the female specialist because of his supposed abilities to deal directly with the creator beings *menemANEn* and *sumInEndu* to elicit their intercession in epidemics, floods, droughts, war, and crop failures. Female specialists are supposed best able to deal with aspects of the supernatural affecting day-to-day events in the crises of birth, illness, death, luck, and so on. A female specialist is believed unable to appeal directly to *menemANEn* and *sumInEndu* because of an inherent female inability to maintain emotional stability in the face of such contacts. In an emergency female specialists can perform rituals primarily undertaken by males.

There are at least 180 separate ritual forms used in Dusun life with 218 names. Some ritual forms consist of recitation in specific order of more than 500 sentence-length lines of special verse. A female specialist knowing only ritual forms more commonly used in dealing with personal crises must remember in proper order of time, sequence, and technique 131 rituals comprising more than 2000 lines of verse. If a female specialist learns forms ideally used by male specialists, she may have a total ritual repertory of more than 3000 verse lines. Male specialists are not expected to know all ritual forms used by females. However, most male specialists know and practice many of the rituals used by females.

Thus, in Dusun society, a ritual specialist most often is a person with a high capacity for learning and retaining an enormous body of ritual language and action. They are typically the most poised persons in crises, and often exercise authority over large areas of the daily life of the people in their communities. Ritual specialists tend usually to be dominant in social situations, assertative and demanding of others, especially with reference to behavior adhering to expected customary uses.

Selection of new female ritual specialists is the result of a formal process, ideally taking place about once in seven years, in which the most respected female specialist of the village urges in public that a number of girls, of 10 to 12 years of age, become learned in ritual belief and acts. A regular series of seven or more special meetings, termed *pEkesusuon,* lasting over a year or more, are held for girls to hear and watch specialists in ritual acts. Half the girls attending sessions of ritual instruction may be children of ritual specialists. Ideally, any girl of "good character" can attend, providing payment of the instruction fee, in the form of chickens, rice, and cloth, is given to the ritual specialist for imparting knowledge of the supernatural.

Meetings of learners are arranged for times of leisure of specialists conducting the training. It is expected each ritual will be learned as taught; when a word is missed in sequence, the verse is begun anew. In between formal sessions of training a girl will practice with other pupils in out-of-the way places, to avoid teasing comment from onlookers. In such practice three or four girls gather in a circle under the edge of a roof overhang of a remote rice storehouse, where they sit and chant each verse to be learned, prompting each other at mistakes in uses or timing. At times of major rituals it is not unusual to see six to ten female specialists prompting each other in a similar manner to avoid "spoiling" the effect of ritual by missed verse. Ideally, a mistake in verse demands restarting of the entire ritual. It is the usual practice, however, to allow the most competent specialist to sing a verse line, with other specialists joining in as a chorus of repetition. No one in Sensuron can remember when a ritual act had to be started again from failure of memory.

A final test of learning is arranged for each girl. Such a test may come at completion of the seven formal sessions of *pEkesusuon,* although most often it occurs after several added years of memorization, practice, and observation of ritual. The test takes the form of a supervised divination and cure of a serious personal illness.

The female specialist is supposed to use a personal, or familiar, spirit as a medium in contacting supernatural forces and beings. Male specialists do not employ a familiar spirit, since they are believed capable of dealing directly with *menemANEn* and *sumInEndu.* A familiar spirit should be acquired by a new ritual specialist at completion of training. In actual practice female specialists reported possession by their familiar spirit from 1 to 12 years after completion of their *pEkesusuon.* The experience of possession was reported by *Kumpiek* in these words:

> I see the familiar spirit in color, as in a dream, and it is a woman like me. When I first was learning to know the ways of the *bElEnketAs* (specialist) I forgot things and missed proper ways. Then one day, while practicing the verses of the *mEgEndi* (a major female ritual), I felt the familiar spirit come into me. She came as a great tingle to my finger tips, like the feeling you get when they go to sleep and then the blood comes back again. That feeling went through my arms to my whole body and I began to shake slowly, then faster and faster as the specialist does when she is possessed by a spirit familiar in a ritual. I shook harder and harder and my head felt light and hot, and my hands grew so heavy that I could not lift them. I saw colors in many mixtures and ways before my eyes and then I grew bigger and bigger until I was a giant. Then that spirit left me and I had a heavy pain in my chest and I was very tired. I could not speak and I had to go down and sleep there on the ground. I knew when I woke that it was my familiar spirit, because she had said the words they say before returning to their dwelling place.

A familiar spirit is acquired for life. It can be invoked only through use of the *kAmbarANun* root in performance of a specific ritual act. When possessed by her familiar spirit and speaking in its voice, the specialist is known as "one who speaks with the voices of the wind, sun, rain, and stars." The familiar spirit is believed to descend and ascend the long stock of the *kAmbarANun* root to the lower and upper halves of the universe in her search for disease givers or souls of the dead responsible for crises. The root is especially cultivated by female specialists and is "brought to life" through a brief ritual, then hung to dry in house eaves. Before the root can be used in major ritual it must be "given the power" through a lengthy formal ceremony. In this act several female specialists participate in recitation of verse and magical acts known to insure power from the plant.

Male ritual specialists are not especially selected, trained, or given special tests of their developing skill. A boy usually selects himself to become knowledgeable in ritual. A typical account is that given by *Dumbor,*

> I learned the rituals when I was a boy of 14 or so. My father and mother became very sick and there was no one to cure them because everyone else in the village had run away from fear of smallpox. There was an old man, named *Deke,* living in a little house in the jungle near the village. So I went to ask him about the sickness of my parents. He told me to sit down and learn the ritual to seek help from the creator, but I fell asleep as he talked. In my sleep I had a dream and I saw the creator who touched my hand and it felt heavy, and I tingled all over, and then the creator told me to wake and I would remember all the rituals needed by a wise *rukeAn* (male specialist). I did, and I could speak all the rituals properly. The next thing, I went home and said the ritual for curing the smallpox and I saved my parents. In four days my parents were well. Many other people came to me and I cured them too. Since then I can talk with the creator whenever there is trouble for our village

Male ritual specialists do not use the *kAmbarANun* root in ritual acts, since they are believed able to "go directly to the creator." Male specialists may, however, use small, oval, flattened stones with stick figures of humans drawn upon them to serve as a means of contact with the creator. Known as "stone children," they are replaced on occasion by small carved and painted wooden human images, or "wood children." Although he may learn female ritual, a male specialist will not acquire a familiar spirit.

Dusun ritual specialists are not expected to be celibates, hermits, or ascetics. Nor are they expected to enhance the efficiency of ritual through personal abasement or material poverty. The abilities and knowledge of ritual specialists make them symbols of normality and stability in a community. When the ritual specialist is healthy, prospers in food and property, and displays good cheer, then it is felt by others that all is in order in the universe.

Religious Practices

Dusun religious practices are to be seen in everyday life in the two general forms of personal action or organized ritual. A substantial portion of religious behavior consists of personal ritual action. Vigorous spitting, with exclamations of *pEtue*! or *ptA*! is a symbol of great personal disgust and is used when any harmful supernatural beings or forces are discussed. When a person working or traveling alone fears supernatural harm, he continually clears his throat and sinuses and then spits vigorously, a sign of rejection of the influence of harmful spirits. Spitting is believed also to fend off disease carried on the first rays of the rising sun. When first leaving the house in the morning it is felt wise to spit gently in the direction of the sun and repeat the phrase, *sElAko mEnukA,* "a greeting to the unfriendly ones from me." This act and phrase are used also as protection against harm carried on the wind and found in the jungle in muddy places and in streams.

At least 20 other personal acts are used in everyday life in Sensuron in efforts to deal by magical behavior with unknown and unseen forces causing fear and harm. The bark of the *tApurau* tree is dried and made into torches and carried at night, for it is believed the pungent odor of the bark drives away the disease giver known as *sedut sedut*. It is believed also that a blade of grass or a small leaf placed on top of the right ear serves as a sign of willingness not to give offense to disease givers.

The bulk of such personal magical practices used by Dusun serve more to align the individual with supernatural forces than provide mastery or control for him in situations causing fear and uncertainty. It is in ritual conducted by male and female specialists that specific attempts are made to control or alter events supposed to be causing the crises of life. These 180 formal practices are grouped by Dusun in 8 general classes of ritual: (1) birth and growth, (2) sickness, (3) death, (4) community safety, (5) agriculture, (6) hunting, (7) luck and fortune, and (8) personal safety from aggression.

The rituals of male and female specialists are comprised of a number of distinct parts that can be used alone or in combination depending on the occasion. The major female specialist ritual form is known as *mEgEndi,* while the major male specialist form is called *renit dE mENeAleg*. Since the *mEgEndi* is used most often in Dusun life, it will be described briefly. The *renit dE mENeAleg* is described in Chapter 5. The *mEgEndi* contains 16 separate ritual acts, while the *renit dE mEneAleg* comprises 19 distinct ritual acts. Each of the separate acts is intended to bring about control or alleviation of a specific crises.

A *MEgEndi* usually consists of five sections, without regard to the number of ritual acts performed in each section. In the first section, termed *narAnki,* or "waking up," the female specialist calls forth her familiar spirit from the *kAmbarANun* root, through running the tip of her right forefinger along the blade of a magically endowed knife. As she moves her finger she chants softly,

> Wake up, sacred plant, wake up!
> Sacred plant, I wake you to tell me,
> I wake you to tell me,
> If I may serve this person?

When the familiar spirit awakes in the *kAmbarANun* root the specialist's finger stops at a point along the blade surface; this point is an indication of the nature of the disease giver or soul of the dead causing the crisis. From this indication the specialist often chooses the types of ritual to be said. The *narAnki* is said while the specialist sits at the side of the afflicted person. Next to the specialist, on the house floor, is a rice sifting tray containing ritual objects and egg, rice, salt, tobacco, and rice wine. There also will be a live pig or chicken laid alongside the ritual objects. Whether a pig or a chicken is used in *mEgEndi* depends on the nature of the crisis. A chicken ideally will be used if the crisis is personal illness sent by a disease giver. If the crisis is suspected as a consequence of violation of fundamental customary behavior, such as incest, then ideally a pig is used. In either instance, use of the animal is a means of "cooling off" the anger of the offended supernaturals. However, decisions regarding use of the pig or chicken in ritual often are made by the family of the affected person; social status in the village is derived from public consumption of such valued goods. When the female specialist uses the chicken, the ritual name changes to indicate the lesser expenditure of goods. When the pig is used, the name of the ritual is altered to note the investment of valued goods.

The second section of the *mEgEndi* is known as *lebabo,* or "going to the creators," and involves three parts. The female specialist begins by making a formal call to the offending spirit or force to stop its harm. Then she calls in turn on each of the 20 disease givers and 20 souls of the dead, through "sending" her familiar spirit to their places of life. Three levels are recoginized as dwelling places of harmful spirits: (1) *sAnhEmbAhEmbA,* or "all spirits wandering the earth"; (2) *kAlEbEnkEn,* or "all spirits under the earth"; and (3) *lAbAbo,* or "all spirits above the earth." Calling the name of each spirit, the specialist inquires in verse, through use of her familiar spirit, whether that spirit has caused the crisis at hand. Failing to obtain an answer from any disease giver or soul of the dead, the specialist calls on each of the 25 spirits of the *kAmbarANun,* asking them through the familiar spirit if they can tell the cause of the crisis. After this lengthy inquiry has failed to produce an answer, the specialist sends the familiar spirit to speak with one of the "lesser" or "lower" creator legend beings. The specific lesser creator being appealed to in *mEgEndi* varies, depending on the nature of the crisis and the preferences of the specialist.

The third section of *mEgEndi* begins when the lesser creator being replies to the entreaty of the specialist. This section, known as *rEndukAn,* or "revelation," is characterized by supposed possession of the body of the specialist by her familiar spirit. Possession, or *gAgarAn,* is believed the sign of the message from the creator being as it is brought by the familiar spirit, and is marked by a shaking of the hands and arms, then the upper body, and finally the entire frame. The tempo of shaking increases slowly at first, but soon reaches a violent crescendo of trembling as the familiar spirit takes over the body of the specialist. At the start of *rEndukAn* the specialist picks up a set of objects, termed *gEndIN,* consisting of metal pieces of valued old gongs and knife blades that are tied with portions of *kAmbarANun* root. As intensity of the possession experience increases the *gEndIN* give off a staccato beat. It is the *gEndIN* which provide a sign that the specialist has found the offending spirit form.

When the offending spirit has been identified through a message from the lesser creator being, the specialist ceases to be possessed, rests briefly, and then undertakes a ritual act to effect a cure. This begins the fourth section of *mEgEndi,* the "ritual of sickness curing." During this period either the chicken or pig are ceremonially cleansed through verse recitation and then given symbolically to the disease giver or soul of the dead to appease its anger. The reason for such a practice is clear in the comment of *Moshi* of Sensuron:

> The animal is given as food for the disease giver. When it has eaten that sweet flesh, it cannot be angry at its host for the meal. It must think better with a full belly, than with an empty one. A full belly keeps the blood busy and out of the heart, so anger is not so easy. When the sick man gives the animal he hopes to make that bad one happy so it forgets its anger and goes away with its sickness.

During this section of *mEgEndi* the ritual specialist may engage in attempts to withdraw objects "thrown into the body" of the victim by the offended spirit. This act involves a separate ritual and the palpation of body parts until pain-causing objects are located and withdrawn from the flesh through pinching or sucking by the specialist. Objects withdrawn are usually small stones, sharp slivers of bamboo and wood, animal bone, or harmful jungle fruit or nuts.

If the ritual used in the fourth section of *mEgEndi* is designed to effect prevention of illness or recover a soul from the land of the dead, object withdrawal is replaced by a long verse form designed to terminate these crises. In either instance Dusun believe a cure or alleviation of a personal crisis derives directly from *kInArINan,* a term used to designate the group of lesser creator beings. Disease and misfortune are not considered to be a property or power of the original creator beings, unless men grossly violate custom. Sickness is known to be caused by a spirit offended by some act of a human in which the supernatural being is injured or its sensibilities offended; thus, in burning a field, a spirit is burned; in crushing a rock, a spirit is crushed; or in disturbing the water, a spirit finds its way disrupted.

The fifth section of *mEgEndi,* "the going up," involves the familiar spirit again taking possession of the specialist. When the state of *gAgarAn* is reached the metal of *gEndIN* again sounds a sharp beat in the shaking hands of the specialist. At the point of intense possession the familiar spirit speaks through the mouth of the specialist, in "a voice of the wind, sun, rain, and stars," saying:

> We go up into the night, we go up to that sacred place.
> We will live quietly.
> We shall be quiet there.

On completion of this verse the effect of possession ceases for the specialist and the ritual of *mEgEndi* is complete, for the familiar spirit has returned to her abode in the *kAmbarANun* root.

A *mEgEndi* is a time of feasting, drinking, and gossip for participants. It is not unusual for such a ritual act to last three to four days, since the amount of time used depends always on skills of the specialist, the nature of the suspected crisis, and the need for consultation with numerous disease givers and souls of the dead, beings of the *kAmbarANun,* and lesser creators. Preparations for *mEgEndi* begin with a decision to try to discover and deal with the nature of a crisis affecting one or several members of a family, and involve the making of rice wine and the gathering of sufficient foodstuffs to provide for all persons asked to attend the ritual. Generally the entire local group of relatives, members of cooperative work groups, and friends are invited to come to *mEgEndi.* In addition, politically powerful persons and ritual specialists from nearby villages often are invited. At a *mEgEndi* given by a wealthy family more than 100 persons may participate as onlookers. The amount of rice consumed in the form of drink and food may equal the entire yearly rice diet of a poor village family. In Sensuron wealthy families organized *mEgEndi* at a ratio of about six to one for poorer families.

It is at times of such organized ritual that the ordinary member of the village knows there are means of controlling unknown and harmful forces. His fears and uncertainty of having to exist with danger and misfortune are reduced considerably through acts of specialists dealing on nearly equal terms with supernatural beings and forces. It is in organized ritual such as *mEgEndi* that belief in a supernatural world is made real for the people of Sensuron, and the crises of life reduced to manageable terms through building barriers of belief against forces of harm.

4

Omens, Luck, and Chance

PERSONAL LUCK is believed by Dusun to shape the ways life crises affect particular persons. There is a great concern in everyday activities with perceiving omens as indications of luck. And there are many ways of ritual behavior and belief in a Dusun village that are special efforts at maintaining and extending luck.

Conceptions of Luck

The people of Sensuron feel each person is born possessed of a store of personal luck. Fortune is supposed given to each person at birth through a specific act of the male creator. Such an award is viewed as the creator's way of indicating the limits of personal fate. *AseNeaE,* a 50-year-old female, noted these things about her luck:

> I had two babies and they both died. So I went to the female ritual specialist. She did a ritual to search out my luck. Then my luck returned to me. I had two more babies and they lived. Luck comes from *menemANEn* (male creator). Not everyone can have luck, for if they did, there would be too many people and not enough food or property for them. So the creator sends bad luck to people to keep the world in balance. He does this in sorrow, for he is kind. When he first made people they were all equal. But *sumAsaui* (beneficial spirit) told the creator that people could not be equal, because no one would know how beautiful, poor, strong, or intelligent they were, so they must be made unequal. So the creator made the differences that exist between men, and he sends these as fortune to each of us when we are born here.

The limit or amount of individual luck is believed measured in the kinds of property acquired in life, success in farming, hunting, and trading, and the successful outcome of personal disputes. The term *naekEt gesAum,* or "to come to limits of luck," is used often to indicate that a person's fortune has failed him. But within the limit of alloted personal luck it is possible through ritual to search out and lure back personal fortune.

Dusun note it is often the case that one or both partners in a marriage are only moderately lucky, but then have a child possessed of extraordinary fortune. When this occurs parents share in the good fortune of the child, and begin to acquire the signs and products of good fortune. It is possible that fortunes of parents are so bad that even when they do produce a lucky child, it will die. When a lucky child dies, luck dies with him, unless it is transferred at death in a special ritual act (see Chapter 5). On occasion, a parent gets to be very boastful concerning change in family fortune brought by the lucky child. At such times it is believed the creator will take back the luck he has bestowed and give it to another family that will not be too proud of its luck.

It is considered unwise to praise the good fortune of others, since such words could be misunderstood by the creator as boasting on the part of a lucky person. If praise is given at all for personal successes, a special term is added after the comment as a means of restoring any damage to good fortune caused another through drawing attention to it. Parents dislike having children praised and will warn another making such comment with the term *orArAn!* (do not bring bad luck!)

Perhaps a greater concern of each Dusun is that a person can be too lucky in one special instance and thereby change the nature of general personal good fortune. Thus a hunter fears catching two animals in one trap, or wounding two animals with one blowpipe dart. A woman gathering fruit is afraid of discovering a tree with an abundance of fruit.

When an individual has such special instances of fortune, they often carefully leave a very conspicious amount of the substance of luck (for example, one animal, or half the fruit) to avoid luck change. Tales of bad fortune often begin with comment regarding personal greed which brought on bad luck.

A conception of reciprocal luck is found in Dusun belief and actions concerned with personal aggression. Arguments between persons, especially adults living in the same neighborhood of a village, most often are concluded through secret attempts at poisoning food or drinks, or in magical acts that represent poisoning, rather than ending in violence with fists or weapons. The intent of most poisoning is to harm health, and thereby luck, rather than to kill. Since most Dusun adults manage to argue violently with several persons in the course of their lives, fears of attempts to poison are a part of everyday village life. Individuals possessed of a great magical strength that protects them against acts of poisoning, or magical efforts to poison, acquire their protection from two sources: they are especially considerate of not harming personal fortunes of others through words or actions, or they have acquired through ritual action a set of magically endowed objects, termed *gemAt,* or a specific medicinal antidote for poisoning called *rusApAn.* The *gemAt* materials usually are hidden on the body to give power against attempts of others to change personal fortune through harmful and magical acts. A female ritual specialist is supposed to make *gemAt* from hair taken from the beard of a soul of the dead, from the heart of a wildcat, and from the brain of the orangutan, among many other things. The antidote of *rusApAn,* usually carried secretly in a small container, is made from the bark of the *pAlu* tree, hornbill bird beak and wing bones, the beak of a crow, a substance from the liver of the porcupine, and "toenails of a rhinoceros."

It was noted in the last chapter that belief in the power of *tApun* is an effective social control device, since generally it prevents persons from refusing food and drinks offered by another because of suspicion of an attempt to poison to alter fortune arising from some past argument or long-term disagreement. However, if a Dusun believes another seeks to harm him, he can refuse food and drink without bringing *tApun* to his host through touching food or drinks with the first finger of the right hand, then touching that finger to the lips or tongue to show symbolic tasting, while saying *tApun oku,* or, "If I caused *tApun* by refusal of your food or drinks, I shall then have it too." Thus personal fortunes are kept generally in reciprocal balance through this device.

Two other beliefs about protection from change in personal luck are used in Dusun life. Most persons engaged in trading goods carry objects, termed *pEININININdApE,* or "lucky property." Most often such objects consist of a small container of coconut oil to make wares "slippery" and thus easily sold for large profit. In contrast to *gemAt* objects, if such items are seen, bad luck will follow. Objects possessed of *gemAt* are believed more powerful if occasionally displayed, for they "bring fear to the heart of the enemy." There also is a belief in *dAp-Euan,* or "restoration of luck with property." If a man is killed in a fight with another member of the village, a hearing is held to judge whether the luck of the deceased had reached its limits. Lengthy testimony is given concerning events indicating the luck of the victim. If it is decided that it was the fortune of the victim to have died in a fight, the murderer is liable to restoration of the luck of the victim's family through payment to the oldest male relative of the dead man's father of specific articles of property in the form of jars, gongs, and animals.

Many everyday activities in a Dusun village include an active concern with personal fortune. It is not unusual, for example, to see a woman sitting on a house porch stringing nearly whole egg shells on pieces of rattan, thereby "increasing the luck from chickens." Such strings are hung in house eaves and serve as a signal to the creators or disease givers, and souls of the dead of a desire to recapture luck in food that has supposedly been lost through some action.

Hunters may sit in the shade of the house after a day in the jungle and make a string of pig skulls or deer skulls in a similar fashion and for the same reason. It is the practice also for trophies of human heads and hands to be tied in strings to the branches of the magically endowed *sEgIndi* tree to increase personal fortune in war (see Chapter 7).

A noticeable aspect of Dusun daily concern with luck comes in conceptions and use of lucky and unlucky numbers. Most ritual acts are conducted with specific reference to monthly and annual calendar numbers; thus, in ritual used after childbirth, the even-numbered days following birth (2d, 4th, 6th, and so on) days are considered "lucky" or "cool" days and proper times for rituals. The odd-numbered days after birth (1st, 3d, 5th, and so on) are "hot" and thus very unlucky days for ritual. Most other ritual acts are conducted on days said to be lucky.

The days of the monthly calendar are arranged in a series of "good-luck" and "bad-luck" days. The 24-day month, which depends on appearance of the moon, is divided into alternating sets of days, in which only certain work activities should be undertaken, and times when it would bring bad fortune to do any work. There are 13 days in each month that are felt to be lucky days, while 11 days are supposed to be so unlucky that only abstinence from work would prevent changes in fortune. In practice, today only two or three bad-luck days (the 15th, 23d, and 24th) are included as times of rest in Sensuron.

While Dusun generally believe even-numbered events or objects in any series are more fortunate than odd-numbered events of a sequence, days of the month also appear to be designated as lucky or not according to association of day names with sounds of other words having unfortunate meanings. So it is said that the 17th day, *kAtAN,* sounds much like the word *lumAtAN,* an expression meaning "to leave out a day," or "a death has occurred," while the 18th day, *kAlintAbAsAn* is said to be similar to the sound of the phrase *kAtAbAs dE tukAd,* "to take away the house steps," meaning that all members of a house have died.

Conceptions of fortune are associated also with repetitions of events or acts. To repeat an action twice is felt very unlucky, while three repetitions are held most fortunate. It is common to hear Dusun say to others, *sAgENun,* "I make it three times," to maintain their fortune as they act. It is usual also to hear the phrase *nAsAgEn-nu?* ("have you tried three lives?") in reply to a comment about personal bad luck. Planting rice is usually done in groups of five seeds, under the belief that a person mentally subtracts four seeds while planting, thereby leaving only one seed, or *tAnsEN,* the lucky single, or "first" number. Generally the lower a number used in any act, the closer it is believed to the magical good fortune of the prime number. The phrase *keuarE tAnsEN,* "the lucky first number," is used to denote belief in magical good fortune coming from use of such a number. Other numbers are felt also to be especially lucky or not; the number seven is believed very lucky, since there are seven souls in good health, while the number eight is considered quite unlucky, since it means "nothing," or "to not exist," for it follows the number seven; the number eight is believed to be the sign of death, or absence of life, since it follows the number for "normal health." The expression *uAlu-ee*!, or "nothing exists there!" (also "death is there!"), is used by people to avoid going along with a group to a place or event they fear or dislike. It is not uncommon to hear one Dusun discourage others from going to a party at a house where they dislike the hosts through saying *uAlu-Amoi*!—"eight are going to that place!" thereby denoting bad fortune or death from attendance.

Omens

There are a variety of occurrences that the people of Sensuron suppose indicate some future change in their personal luck. These signs of future events are termed *kopeAn,* or "omens," and are found in at least four different kinds of events: (1) The sights and sounds of different animals are portents of future events. (2) Finding objects also heralds changes in luck. (3) The sight of falling objects give auguries of things to come. (4) Dreams reveal events that foretell the future luck of individuals.

Omens are believed to forecast the specific nature of personal health, including major sickness and death. No major activity is undertaken without consultation of appropriate signs of the future. All agricultural, hunting, and building activities have specific omens associated with their success or failure. Travel and trading is not undertaken without detailed attention to signs that are supposed forerunners of things to come. Warfare is conducted only with specific attention to omens of success in personal safety and great victories.

Foremost among Dusun omens are the sights and sounds of particular birds. Dusun know and name 95 of the more than 500 species of birds now recognized in Borneo. The principal birds giving omens are the rufous and buff-necked woodpecker, the grey-and-buff woodpecker, or fulvous rumped barred woodpecker, the maroon woodpecker, the speckled piculet and malaysian pygmy pied woodpecker, common and forest kingfishes, the white-breasted waterhen, the malaysian eagle-owl, the brahminy kite, and a variety of the hornbills, including the white-crested hornbill, the wreathed hornbill, the black hornbill, the helmeted hornbill, and the rhinoceros hornbill. Birds are said to tell of the future because of events that took place at the time of creation.

Since the nature of upper jungle vegetation makes the sighting of many omen birds difficult, their sounds have also come to have meanings as indicators of fortune. One call of any of the woodpeckers is taken as a sign of impending death. Two cries of any woodpecker indicates sickness in the future, three cries a misfortune, while four cries of this bird denotes future good luck. If a lone traveler in the jungle should hear a buff-necked woodpecker call four times and then hears four calls of the grey-and-buff woodpecker it is a most fortunate omen, for doubling of the calls is known as a sign that the creator specially aids luck.

In addition to birds, there are at least 12 other animals whose sight or sounds give omens of fortune, including bats, rats, deer, millepedes, centipedes, civets, snakes, dogs, otter, chameleons, frogs, and pigs. Generally, sight or sound of any of these animals is considered a bad omen at the start of a journey, the building of a house, or in trading goods.

The sight, sound, or a combination of sights and sounds in one day of a set of three animal omens denotes impending sickness, loss of property, and death.

Indications of future luck also are taken by Dusun from accidental finding of certain objects and from sight of certain falling objects. If, on a journey or during a hunt or work in the jungle, a person comes upon a clear, bright stone, the future of the finder is supposed to be bright and unclouded. Similarly the finding of particular animal remains, such as a hornbill beak, rhinoceros horn, or pig incisors, is a lucky omen. There are a number of objects whose sight, when falling, are omens of bad luck. If a large jungle tree falls, there is to be sickness and misfortune ahead. The sight of a green tree limb crashing to the jungle floor is a precursor of falling and breaking a limb, or a general fall in personal fortune.

To avoid sights of unlucky omens or contact with omen animals while on a journey, travelers usually engage in a ritual termed *pEbuEbur,* "to ask omens for signs of luck." It is believed this inquiry will provide information concerning unfavorable omens. Most Dusun find it necessary to begin long and difficult trips to unfamiliar places at least twice, and will delay or cancel any trip when omens on a second start are unlucky.

It is believed generally that in sleep the final soul wanders about in the future; hence dreams are experiences souls have in events that will occur in a time to come.

The wanderings of the soul in dreams are supposed not to be controlled by ritual or magical act. When a person has trouble, Dusun may say, "I don't know what my soul has done," or "I do not wish to do these things, but my soul has gone there and it has happened to me." It is a sound legal defense to note that personal behavior is the product of, and depends upon, the experiences of the soul in dreams.

The types of events considered ill omens in dreams do not necessarily correspond to belief and behavior in omen taking in daily life. So dependence on sights and sounds of animals, and particularly birds, in taking indications of future luck is not reflected generally in dream content. On inquiry Dusun say simply that "the soul does things without control—you do not have to go out and see omens."

While interpretation of dream omens vary from time to time, and often with immediate personal concerns of the dreamer, the people of Sensuron agree that certain interpretations could generally be placed on dream events. As examples, falling trees indicate death, while dreams of a setting sun at a particular distance above the horizon foretells the time in years until death; one measure above the horizon, termed *tepAN seku* (distance from middle finger tip to elbow), equals one year of remaining life. People frequently dream they see the sun seven measures above the horizon. A dream of the sun below the horizon denotes the placement of a body in the grave, while dreams of losing a hat indicate loss of a head in war. A dream of a house on fire means sickness with high fever. Dreaming of ants carrying a burden or a burden on a pole is an indication of death, for bodies are carried to the grave slung under a pole. Dreams of intercourse with a relative or a friend's husband or wife are omens of a horrible death from epidemic disease.

Dreams are believed vital also in Dusun life as means of expressing *Erul genauE,* or "a wish of the mind." When a dream is recounted that is more complex than a straight forward account of seeing one event, listeners know they hear of troubles caused by not only the soul's wanderings, but also the wishes, desires, and guilt of the soul. The following text of a dream, given by a 23-year-old female, clearly expresses *Erul genauE:*

> A woman from Patu was on her way to Ranau and she heard two omens. In her sleep she had a dream of intercourse with her father. When she woke she was afraid and returned home. When she returned home she was very

sick. Her mother told her she was sick because the creators would most certainly kill any girl guilty of incest. The girl did not know her father, who lived in another village. Her father and mother had divorced before that girl was born, and so she had never seen her father. She did not know whether he was alive. Then she recovered and went again to Ranau. On her way she passed through a village where she met a kind and handsome man, and she loved him and had intercourse there. Then she went on her way. She had many bad omens, and so she returned home, stopping again to have intercourse with the man. One day after she came home she died; that man was her own father, and she had done *sEmbAN* (incest) twice. It was not her fault, for mothers always point out to daughters their fathers are dead when they divorce that way. The girl thought her father dead. It was her soul's wishes in the dream that made her have intercourse. She should have heeded the dream and understood that it told of the unnatural longing of the soul.

Omens and luck are among prime topics of everyday conversation for the people of Sensuron. Casual or small talk of any extended time usually will contain substantial amounts of trading of omens seen or avoided, and reports of omens and luck of others in the village or area. Some joking takes place in such discussion, with comments such as, "you couldn't see well enough to know that omen!" However, such discussions are conducted usually in a manner in accord with the belief that luck and its indications, even for others, is a most important matter.

5

Sickness and Death

THE PEOPLE of Sensuron feel that the state of the universe as well as omens of personal fortune are responsible for sickness. The condition of a "hot universe" (*AlAsu dE pEmEgEnA*) is feared greatly since at such a time the "fever of sickness" afflicts man, plants, and animals. When the universe is *AsAgit,* or "cool," then it is believed personal fortunes will be good and men can expect to be in good health and live to the limits of their fate.

Sickness

Dusun use more than 109 specific terms in their concerns with sickness. These terms vary from general body part detail such as chest (*kAnkAb*) and blood (*rAhA*) to colors of skin in conditions of health and sickness.

At least 60 kinds of disease, or conditions, are recognized in Sensuron. Disease classifications are complex since the nature of treatment by ritual and specific medicines, as well as whether the ill person survives, may often determine the ways sickness is finally classed.

A British medical officer stationed at Keningau, some 70 miles south of the Sensuron, made monthly visits to the Tambunan government station in 1959–1960. The medical officer's reports of treatment of Dusun patients seen for the first time, either as outpatients or as hospital patients, provide some indication of the nature of illness and accident encountered in a Dusun community. A total of 42,928 patients, seen over a three-year period (1959–1962), were classed by four medical officers in these ways: infections and parasitic diseases, 10,204; respiratory diseases, 8385; gastrointestinal diseases, 3646; diseases of skin and connective tissue, 3596; musculoskeletal diseases, 2155; diseases of the eye, 1712; blood and lymphatic diseases, 1636; ear, nose, and throat diseases, 1490; dental and oral diseases, 1125. Thirteen other disease classes accounted for 1407 patients, including gynecologic and obstetric disease (454), allergies (260), metabolic diseases (216), and cardiovascular diseases (98). There were 62 cases of neuropsychiatric disorders and 22 instances of diagnoses of malignant neoplasms, or cancers. Among the nearly 43,000 patients, 2928 were victims of accidents, poisoning, or wounds from assaults. The remainder of the patients were ill of diseases so ill-defined due to lack of clear symptoms and inadequate diagnostic facilities that they were unclassified. The statistics of disease given here must be qualified by the fact that most patients seen by medical officers are usually very ill and fear death more than they do the hospital and Western custom. And most suffered from several diseases; the data collected by the colonial service required reporting of only one disease per patient. Most adults treated for any reason, including accidents, had multiple intestinal parasites, were moderately to severely anemic, and often suffered nutritional and metabolic diseases and some form of eye and skin infections.

Disease and Population

In the time from September 1959 to September 1960 Sensuron had a population of 947 persons regularly in residence in the village. Census counts taken in October 1959 and August 1960 provide a record of reported ages of village residents. The age structure of the village reflects markedly at least two of several factors affecting life in Sensuron, a high birth rate and a high death rate. In 1959–1960 44 babies were born in Sensuron, including two sets of twins. Approximately 49 percent of the total population were children under 16 years of age.

The number of deaths from all causes in Sensuron in 1959–1960 totaled 18 persons, including 8 adult males, 3 adult females, 4 boys, and 3 girls. In the same period 10 of the 44 babies born died from sickness.

The Dusun conception of pain includes both physical pain and pain caused by gossip. The term, *tarErul* is used to designate a distressing feeling from illness and uneasiness and anguish from being maligned or slandered. The most severe pain is said to come from aggression by gossip. Sharp pains in the chest are usually attributed to the unkind words of someone bearing malice toward another. Human feces and urine also are felt dangerous because they cause serious illness, with disabling pains. An initial reaction to sharp pain, not localized in a specific body part, is to suspect contamination from feces or urine. The comment is often heard, "I have been sick since I smelled those feces." A common act of covert aggression is to take fecal matter and rub it secretly on house posts to bring pain to its inhabitants.

A cowardly act is excused if the smell of *tie,* or feces-urine, is claimed, for it is accepted that a person becomes nervous from being made ill by such odors.

Maintenance of personal health is believed also to depend on not being hurt accidentally by sickness thrown at someone else by a disease giver or a soul of the dead. To insure health at least five specific practices are followed. The carrying of a magic object (*gEmAt*) makes a person invincible to sickness. The wearing of small bits of *kAmborANun* root on the clothing is believed to frighten away disease givers and souls of the dead by the smell of the plant. An application to the head of a poultice made of beeswax and plant materials, termed *pulesEk* or *sApenIt,* is believed to make the wearer invisible. A container of water, made potent through special ritual, termed *pEpEdsu,* is carried to make the body slippery in the grasp of disease givers and souls of the dead. Finally, seeds from the *delai* plant, strung as beads, are worn as a bracelet or necklace because the name of the plant is similar to the word *mEgAli* or "to avoid." Thus the person wearing the beads becomes *Aliaun,* "one who avoids sickness." In times of illness affecting numbers of people in a village, one or all of these magical charms are worn by adults. Children under the age of two years wear *delai* all the time, and have regular applications of *pulesEk* made to their beads to cover the *tImpEruru,* or "spot of soul exit."

Relief of sickness is attempted in two general forms other than the ritual act of *mEgEndi.* First, a variety of plant substances are used to treat illness and to provide immunity to specific diseases. Secondly, particular ritual acts, usually done by a female specialist, are employed to divine the nature of illness and to effect its cure.

At least 80 plants are used by Dusun as treatments for sickness. Plant juices are drunk as medicines and plant fibers are applied as pallatives to wounds, burns, fractures, and sprains.

In addition to these medicines, a series of seven ritual acts, usually termed *mENemuhau* ("to sweep away"), are used to deal with any illness, but especially those concerned with madness, critical infections, "sickness" of rice or other crops, domestic animals, and diseases affecting households but not the neighborhood or village.

The *mENemuhau* rituals are among those forms most commonly seen in daily life in Sensuron, and the verses are those most generally known by persons not specializing in ritual knowledge.

When villagers begin to recover from illness of any type, they are considered to be in a special state, termed *AbenlausEn,* or "to have great desire for food." Food, including rice wine, is considered to restore a victim of disease to his former good health. The general test of good health is whether a person can eat at any time he is offered food; refusal of food is considered a symbol of impending death, since only the dying will not eat.

Sickness and Male Ritual Specialists

At times of community-wide crises, from disease or because of a "hot" universe, ritual action is often undertaken by a male specialist to alter events. Some similarities and differences in selection, training, knowledge, and behavior of male and female specialists in ritual have been noted in preceding chapters. An important difference between the specialists in ritual exists in the fact that when a male specialist deals with a crisis, it is most often a concern with epidemic sickness or disaster affecting great numbers of persons.

The male ritual specialist is believed to call directly to the creator. In such a call the male specialist does not use the *kAmbarANun* plant, a familiar spirit, or engage in possession ritual. Contact with the creator is made through spirit objects, in the form of stone or wood figures, or in the use of plant parts such as the heart of the young banana plant. The banana "heart" is thought to be a symbol of the "earth's heart," and is believed most effective of the three symbols used in calls to the creator.

The major ritual act of the male specialist, *renit dE mENeAleg,* consists generally of three parts. In the initial act, most often carried out in private at the village edge, symbols of magical protection (termed *tINAleg*) are carved from bamboo or wood and empowered to act as "warriors" to war and guard against disease and ill-fortune. When completed they are carried to the village and placed at a point near the main entrance to the community.

Here the second part of the ritual is conducted, with usually a substantial number of the villagers in attendance. At the outset of this second portion of the ritual four special *tINAleg* sticks are set upright in the ground. Then a small elevated and roofed platform is constructed as a focal point of ritual. One or more oval stones are placed in the ground in front or beneath the structure, to "hold down" the principal spirits of the underworld until the male specialist can proceed to make a magical wall of stone about the village to keep out sickness or misfortune.

After selecting and placing the ritual objects, the male specialist begins his call to the creators in these words:

> I shake the earth to awaken the spirits! The underground spirits reply: "Great one, why do you shake the earth?" I reply, I am shaking the earth, because I must make a defense for my world, for we worry about the sickness about to come here, a sickness of many guises and actions; sometimes it follows the wind, other times it follows the paths made by men.
>
> That sickness hunts for the souls of man, a sickness without name, without form, so terrible in its actions. We cannot keep it out, so you spirits of the earth must come out and help build our defenses against the sickness. Let us build a wall of stone from your place up to the sky; let us build it double thick and seven times and about the whole world.
>
> I ask this to keep out the nameless, formless, horrible sickness. Help us!

During the remainder of the ritual the specialist sits with eyes closed, hands held loosely over his knees and face often tilted upward, while calling out ritual verse describing the journey and conversations of the object spirits as they go to the abode of the creator.

After the call of the specialist has been delivered by the object spirits to the creator, the third part of the *renit dE mENeAleg* begins. In this act various ritual forms are said that the creators have indicated as cures for a "hot universe" or ill-fortune. One or several of these rituals may be said to alter the crisis. When all possible forms are included in the third part of the ritual the entire act may take from three to five days, depending on the skills and strength of the male specialist. In longer rituals female specialists may act as a companion to support the verse recitations of the male specialist. It is rare that a second male specialist would join in support of the first, for it is believed their powers would come in conflict and cause harm. Relations between male specialists are tinged with some humor and marked by jokes concerning each others mistakes. Typically, one specialist will seek out another after some natural event of minor effect (a rainstorm, for example,) and joke that the first specialist must have forgotten part of his last ritual. The third part of the ritual involves usually a ceremonial killing of a chicken as a symbol of appeasement of the creators.

Offerings are also made of rice, rice wine, tobacco, and salt. The *renit dE mENeAleg* is concluded when the ritual specialist, after a special verse, takes the smallest of *tINAleg* sticks and throws it toward the village entrance as a warning to spirits ready to attack the community. Then the other *tINAleg* sticks are passed to heads of various families for use at the foot of the house steps to guard the family in the crisis of a hot universe. Finally, the male specialist may place a special *tINAleg,* with its tip carved to a spear point, in the middle of the main path. The spear tip is inclined to the village entrance as the weapon to be used by spirits of the *tINAleg* to fight disease givers. Ideally it is the practice that while this special *tINAleg* is in place no one is permitted to enter or leave the community.

In November of 1959 Sensuron was "walled off" by a *tINAleg* for two days because of fears of a typhoid epidemic reported more than 100 miles to the south. Two visitors who came at that time from distant villages were fined one chicken, one measure of rice, two Malay dollars, and a pack of salt after a hearing by the village headman.

A *renit dE mENeAleg* usually occurs in a day period, with carving of the *tINAleg* taking two hours or so, the *loEn,* or call to the creator, occupying three to five hours, and the ritual acts to effect cure, or alleviation taking between three and six hours. The ritual sequence ordinarily starts in the early morning, at an hour after sunrise to avoid disease givers of the sun and wind, and will be completed prior to sunset, to keep the ritual from being spoiled by disease givers and souls of the dead lurking in the night.

Performance of *renit dE mENeAleg* is a time of solemnity in a Dusun village. Events leading to the need for such a ritual are of such serious nature that few persons are inclined to be festive, as in anticipation of *mEgEndi.* There is always a time of feasting for participants in *renit dE mENeAleg,* but only after completion of the ritual. A major difference in attitudes toward the two major ritual forms is found in the behavior of participants; at times of *mEgEndi* onlookers laugh readily, gossip, and engage in much good-humored practical joking while the female specialist works. The crowd observing the male specialist stands or sits quietly, occasionally talking in casual tones, but without much humor, and little joking. A *renit dE mENeAleg* is not a time of public display of wealth and power, nor a means of securing greater personal or family prestige. Attitudes concerning major rituals of the male and female specialists could be said to be comparable in that they are both means of reducing fears of the unknown through ritual act. But the social functions of the two rituals diverge widely in the differences exhibited between the cheerful and high-spirited occasion of a *mEgEndi* and the tone of personal melancholy, sadness, and air of dread obtaining during *renit dE mENeAleg.*

Death

Few events in the lives of the people of Sensuron bring to focus more of the beliefs and acts concerned with the nonnatural world than does death of a family member. Death is considered a topic most difficult to discuss, conceive, or deal with in any sense. This attitude is summarized in the comment of *Moshi:* .

> Everyone is afraid of death and fears to talk about it. Yet we must prepare for it because it causes great changes in things. But how can we do that, for death is such a terrible event?

Preoccupation with omens of death is great, however, and a matter of immediate interest of everyone whenever the subject is mentioned.

At the obvious approach of death in a critically ill person the father, or the oldest male relative of the father's generation, such as the father's brother, sends for all relatives to witness the death. Dusun say that when death nears quick random motions of hands and eyes foretell the event, for such acts are those of the "overburdened" person who "carries death as a heavy load on his back." When such motions cease death is supposed to be near. The ill person is then usually propped up by being held from behind, as a close relative holds the palms of both hands tightly over the point at the top of the head where it is believed the last soul leaves when breath stops. This point is also a main point of entrance of sickness into the body. When breathing stops, the person holding up the deceased begins to blow his breath on this point to bring warmth and thus life to the body. The deceased is sometimes laid down and covered with as many items of clothing available as a means of keeping warmth and life in the body. Breath is also blown onto the palms of the deceased until they grow cold to the touch. While the body is warm but breathing has ceased, a special state of being, *kApAtiEn,* is recognized for the deceased. Death is socially real and emotionally recognized only after the state of *kApAtiEn* has been passed through, and another state of being, known as *poinpAti,* or "dead," is decreed through start of ritual wailing by relatives. Wailing during the *kApAtiEn* is believed to prevent a return to life should the death be a "mistake" of the creator, that is, a misreading by the creator of the limits of the deceased's fate.

When the body grows cold the social fact of death is recognized and announced by the father of the deceased or the oldest male relative present, through the use of one of two precise expressions translated as, "he exists nomore" or "someone has gone far away." After this announcement ritual wailing begins. At the same time a signal of death is given the community and area through use of gongs beaten in slow unison. In Sensuron wailing immediately after death of a parent is carried out by close family members and usually starts with a mournful cry of *edi oi! edi oi!* (Mother there!), or *AmA oi! AmA oi!* (Father there!). This particular chant proceeds until most close relatives have exhausted themselves. Tears and facial expressions of grief are used generally by women in wailing. Men can wail and show grief through tears, but are believed most often to be so grieved that only a long, low moan of *oooE! oooE!*

can indicate the dimensions of their sorrow. When family members grow exhausted from wailing, several groups of females, comprised of distant relatives and neighbors assemble about the body, sitting in a circle, where they continue wailing. Ideally one person must wail all the time before burial. This form of wailing is often done in close part harmony and consists of detailed recitations of good deeds of the deceased. Wailing begins with a sister or daughter crying out from a distant part of the house the stylized expression, "You have worked so hard in the fields for us, why did you have to die?"

Then an accounting of good works of the dead person is given in turn by each woman seated about the body. Older women use a ritual expression during their mourning, "What can we do, for death is the way of man?" This phrase is intended to console the grieving family, for it denotes the naturalness of such an event. Persons entering the house at the time of the funeral use this expression in greeting relatives of the deceased. The wailing also often includes the phrase, "You who have been bereaved, must eat!" It is believed that persons in deep mourning will not want to eat, and thus will grow thin and ill themselves. Tales of persons dying of grief are common at times of death. A common treatment for deep grief is to keep the lamenting person drunk to cause him hunger and to keep him healthy until his *aupus,* or "missing," grows old with time.

When the initial wailing begins and the gongs begin to sound news of death, the oldest male relatives and close friends of the deceased, whether male or female, gather in front of the house to plan the burial. Burial is always held "a day later from death" and according to a specific schedule of time to provide the dead with "one last night of sleep at home." Burial on the same day of death is greatly feared, for it is believed that men have been buried alive because of inability of relatives to tell from physical signs whether they were alive or dead.

With a decision made on the time of burial the male relatives and friends consult on the problem of *parEndEnEn,* or "goods for the grave." It is customary that animals be killed to accompany the deceased on his trip to the land of the dead, and that certain goods be left at the grave for his uses. The expenses of the funeral in food and drink must also be met from the property left by the deceased. The assembled male relatives and friends take careful verbal inventory of property and then make a choice of kinds and amounts of property to be devoted to the burial and funeral celebration. A very poor person of good reputation may have one of these relatives or friends donate property for use in *parEndEnEn,* with repayment without interest due at some later time. As basic items of *parEndEnEn* one large pig must usually be killed and one medium-size jar be used at the grave. A wealthy person may have one or several *kerabau* (water buffalo) and several large jars used for burial. Choices of other goods, in the form of gongs, weapons, clothes, beads, and tools, are decided on the basis of the question, "What can the family afford to send with the dead, and what must they use themselves?"

While these matters are being settled, one of the male relatives returns to the house to see that the body has been laid out properly for the next form of wailing ritual. The deceased usually has a fresh sleeping plank or mat placed beneath him, and is laid flat on his back, arms folded across the chest. A cloth cover is pulled over the entire body. Before leaving to rejoin the group outside, a male relative often takes a broom and places it briefly in the hands of the deceased, to symbolically "sweep the sky clear of rain." Rainfall during wailing or burial is considered a most unfortunate event, for it brings wet earth, and with such conditions, disease givers and souls of the dead are sure to gather. A polite way of telling another person of death in a community is to use the expression "that one now sweeps the sky clear."

During the hours of discussion by male relatives and friends the topic of a burial party is brought up and after brief mention is passed over for other topics. Men will not work in a burial party willingly, especially if their wives are pregnant, if there is illness in their own immediate family, or if there is a new house to be moved into in the near future.

The final choice of men to comprise the burial party usually is the result of the prestige of the senior male member of the group being brought to bear on four or five men judged to have the fewest reasons for avoiding the task. Members of burial parties are paid a ritual fine (*sAgIt*) of chickens, rice, and salt to separate them from the dead after burial; it is believed the deceased is so grateful for the kindness shown by the burial party that he will want them as company in the land of the dead.

In the hour before burial the face of the dead person is bathed, his hair is combed, and his best clothes are used to dress the corpse. This preparation is done by the oldest child for a parent, or by a father for a child, or by any other relative or person with a "great feeling" for the deceased. Women usually prepare the bodies of young children for burial. After these preparations are completed, the body is lifted and carried to a point near the house entrance. Close relatives gather about the body while the oldest male relative takes the right hand of the deceased, lifts it up, and shakes it sharply several times, so the hand appears to be dropping an object. As this act occurs, the senior male relative says loudly, "I shake the good luck from you to others!" Other members of the family then take the hand of the deceased in turn while repeating this expression, hoping to bring about transfer of good fortune from the deceased to their lives.

At the time agreed upon the body is lifted and placed between two sections of split bamboo, which are bound together and tied to a wood-carrying pole. When this task is completed, all persons present for the burial assemble quietly in the house, sitting or standing close about the walls. Then a large gong is beaten in slow time as a signal of the burial, and the closest female relative—a wife, mother, grandmother, or aunt—begins the final form of wailing by a soaring cry of grief and then a description of her sense of loss. At a burial in Sensuron the wife cried out,

> You have died now, and there is no one to help me! I am so grieved. I do not know how I can live. I do not know how to be a father to our children. Oh, your sickness is so terrible, and I'm so afraid. Do not go there, to the place of the dead. Come back to us.

As this first cry of grief is given, others join in, giving rise to a harmony-like roar of grief, in which individual words are drowned out in a rising and falling crescendo of sounds. Within a few moments the drum of sound subsides and individual female voices can be distinguished calling grief in a tone believed to be similar to that of the music of the *turare* (bamboo flute); it is hoped the wailing will be so "beautiful" that the deceased will want to return to life and friends.

As the burial party lifts the body, everyone present pounds their feet or hands sharply on the floor, as children do in a temper tantrum, as a sign of great grief; female members of the family often throw and break valuable objects, while men may take up spears and hurl them across the house into the wall, shouting, "If this wall is the disease giver that killed you, I kill him!" As the body is carried down the house steps, the wailing, pounding, and hurling of objects rises to a peak and then suddenly dies down completely to silence, except for the stiffled sobs of close female relatives. No one follows the body to the grave.

The burial party carries the body to a site at the edge of the village regularly used for burials. It is considered a mark of disrespect to put the body down during this trip. A grave has been dug some hours previously. At the graveside it has been customary that the body be transferred for burial to a large earthenware jar. Poorer families, unable to afford a jar of this size, must bury the dead in the bamboo covers placed over the body for transport to the grave. No burials in Sensuron in 1959–1960 were in jars. The jar used for burial is 2 feet in diameter at the mouth, 3 feet at midsection and 4 to 6 feet high. The body is placed inside the jar feet first, then lowered, and the arms folded across the chest and inside the knees, which are flexed beneath the chin. Thin, small *parEndEnEn* items are placed inside the jar, and it is closed with a special gong that is placed on the jar as a lid. Before closure a 15-to-20-foot piece of rattan is placed in the right fist of the body to insure that the deceased can signal his return to life while being buried. The end of the rattan line then is led up through the earth and laid on the ground at the head of the grave. Once the grave is filled in, the rattan line is drawn slowly out of the grave, while a ritual is said by the oldest member of the burial party "to draw back the spirits of the living" accidentally left in the grave during burial.

When this ritual is completed the oldest member of the burial party picks up a piece of bamboo or wood from the ground, kneels, and slowly cuts it to a sharp point, as he says the ritual of *pEnEnEnEndEk dE lebAN,* or "to give the power of *tAnduk* to the grave," an act intended to protect the body from the ravages of the souls of the dead.

On completion of this ritual the burial party bathes in the river, changes clothes, and then returns to the deceased's home. Here food is served to the party, apart from the others attending the funeral, and a female specialist does a brief ritual, cleansing the burial party members of bad luck that may come from participation in the funeral and graveside activities.

After burial is completed there is a period of six days in which no work should be undertaken, except for preparation of food. However, during planting and harvest times, and other work emergencies, this period of time can be condensed by counting daylight as equal to "one day" and night as equivalent to "one day." Thus, three days serve as the six-day period of idleness after burial. On the evening of the sixth day after death, which is reckoned as "the seventh night of death," a special ritual observance, called *mEnEmpEle,* is held to note the time when the soul of the deceased is supposed to return to the household for possessions needed in the land of the dead.

Observance of *mEnEmpEle* begins before noon of the sixth day after burial with construction of a structure covering the grave site. Such structures may be a simple roof of bamboo set on four hardwood cornerposts, or elaborate imitations of houses, carefully decorated and carved. In most instances the grave structure is somewhere between these extremes, since prestige depending on the structure's appearance is involved for family members. But, costs of elaborate construction can detract so heavily from the deceased's estate that most families try to avoid detailed carving and decorations. Another substantial expense of *mEnEmpEle* is the animals that must be killed to "accompany" the deceased to the land of the dead. Costs of the sixth day-seventh night observance are raised significantly when costs of animal sacrifice and grave structure are added to the costs of property to be placed inside the grave structure for the soul's use in the land of the dead. If valuable gongs, jars, weapons, tools, and clothes are left at the grave, the estate of the deceased is considerably reduced in value, since these materials can have no value once used on a grave.

After the grave structure is completed and animal remains and goods are placed on top of the grave, the working party, comprised of senior male relatives and friends of the deceased, returns to the house of the bereaved family. Here food and drinks are served, and about sunset a special feast of the "best" foods is prepared and carried by the closest relatives to the grave site. This act is accompanied by a ritual cursing the soul of the dead to warn it from the household.

Returning to the house the relatives sit in the dark with friends and neighbors of the deceased, and wait out the night of *mEnEmple.* Sitting in darkness insures that the soul of the deceased will not be frightened. Although the soul has been cursed from visiting the house, all present know, and expect, it will visit for the night, doing familiar things and lamenting its lost life; those present know when the soul has arrived, for they hear water slashing about in the bamboo water carrier as it takes a drink, and makes noises as it goes about opening boxes looking for favored items of clothing, all the while coughing and breathing in a "tired" manner. After collecting goods left in the house, the soul returns to the grave site, packs up the goods there, and then sets off on the return journey to the land of the dead.

There is disagreement among the people of Sensuron over the activities of a soul after burial and before its return at *mEnEnpEle* time. Some 10 percent of the village adults believe the soul stays quietly near the house until the seventh night. Most village adults believe the soul goes from the grave to a "resting place" near the top of Mt. Kinabalu and then returns for *mEnEmpEle.* There is general agreement that the physical remains of the dead are carried off after burial, once the soul has left the body.

Soul Concepts

In Sensuron it is the belief that each person is born with seven souls, which range in size from the thickness of the thumb to that of the little finger. The souls are believed contained one inside the other and to grow as the body grows. The six outside souls are often designated collectively by the term *mAgalugulu,* "to go on ahead to the place of the dead," after the belief that a soul "runs away from the body" when it is stricken by serious illness and proceeds to *pENAluAn,* "the place of the dead." The cause of some sickness is believed the result of a soul's struggle to be free of the body of a person committing offenses against the creator. Other illness is explained as the attempt of a soul to flee harm by an angry disease giver. After leaving the body all souls except the seventh, or *gAdAgAdA,* can be seen as a fleeting shadow in the shape of a human. The last soul cannot be seen for it has no shape. There are many tales told in Sensuron of individuals seeing one of their souls going on ahead of them to the land of the dead.

When the final soul leaves the body and has collected its goods for the after life in *pENAluAn,* it travels to a resting place for souls near the top of Mt. Kinabalu. Here the soul rests from the wearying journey and talks with other souls enroute to the land of the dead. The final resting place of souls is supposed somewhere beyond Mt. Kinabalu. The afterworld is described in various ways. Typical of such comment is this description by Dao of Sensuron:

> It is a broad level plain. All the houses are new, and the animals there are fat and well fed. There is no sickness, and aways food in abundance. No one fights, or says unkind words and all are happy and content. No one worries about bad luck or omens, and no one fears starvation. All the people are young and beautiful again, and with their families, as in the other times.

Souls of the dead do not all go to *pENAluAn* since some are prisoners of disease givers and others have been captured by harmful souls of the dead. A soul that enters the body of a living person to capture his final soul is regarded as "a spirit of the dead." Such capture causes serious illness and, usually, death.

There are contrasting attitudes in Sensuron regarding the relative seriousness of sickness and death. Illness is much too important a matter in Dusun life for joking. In the broadest sense disease is considered a matter of profound importance, while as a social fact, death is beyond importance because it is a part of the natural order. Thus, after the fact, death can be joked about and be a point of practical jokes; at one Sensuron funeral a close friend of the deceased got beneath the house floor and suddenly raised the body to nearly upright position by use of two sticks, bringing the circle of mourners to a startled halt in their wailing. The joker later was asked by the village headman to pay a fine of one chicken to "cool" his offense against the relatives of the deceased, who were embarrassed because the joker had revealed that the deceased had not been properly dressed in his newest clothing. The fine was not for disrespect to the dead or death, but because of social embarrassment caused the living. Later the joker was the target of a practical joke involving the body of an elderly male who was being carried to the burial area. As the burial party went past the joker's house a relative of the deceased in the first instance called out the joker's name in the falsetto tone supposed used by disease givers. When the joker came to the door, the relative of the first deceased took the hand of the corpse from the bamboo covering and waved a "good-bye" to the joker. No fine was asked for this act, since it was considered a fair return for the "impatience" of the joker in "raising the dead." No one could remember a situation when comparable jokes or joking occurred during sickness. Nor could the people of Sensuron speculate easily on the matter of jokes concerning the illness of others.

However, while death can be made a subject of practical jokes, it is rarely discussed or mentioned in everyday conversation. But illness, which no one seems to feel a joking matter, is a prime topic of daily discussion. These contrasting attitudes regarding illness and death appear to derive from the belief of the people of Sensuron that once death has occurred little can be done to change the event, while illness is a matter that may sometimes be within the comprehension of at least specialists in ritual.

6

Social Relations

DUSUN ARRANGE RELATIONSHIPS with one another according to a set of customary patterns that provide generally for most daily social events and the tasks of living in the Borneo mountain jungle.

Territorial Divisions

The basic social unit in Sensuron is comprised of a compact nuclear family household. Each nuclear family household consists usually of a father, a mother, and their dependent children, and may also have as members a newly married son and his bride, or an aged grandparent, uncle, or aunt, or even a close friend of a grandparent who has no relatives to look after them in old age. In 1959–1960 the average size of a Sensuron nuclear family household was 5 persons, with a range of from 2 to 13 persons.

The village consists of 183 nuclear family households. These households are grouped in five large territorial divisions called *koboginan.* Each division is marked by irregular boundaries formed through a significant feature of the landscape.

The *koboginan* do not appear to control marriage relationships, do not regulate inheritance of property, and have no general economic or major political functions. They do serve as the basis for intermittent performance of ritual celebrating the taking of head and hand trophies in war conducted by men of the *koboginan.*

Within each *koboginan* there are one or several territorially based mutual-aid groupings or *megita.* When an individual aids others in any form of work he expects to be repaid measure for measure. Thus, assistance given in harvesting rice is measured by the number of baskets of rice cut, and a similar amount of help is repaid by a person from the nuclear family household receiving help. A record is kept by making knots on a piece of rattan or by cutting notches in a basket. Nuclear families exchanging mutual aid in work regularly participate in ritual feasting on occasion of the major work activities of harvest, house building, and clearing of land. The feasting often leads participants in labor exchange to consider themselves relatives. Children of individuals belonging to the same *megita* are said ideally to be related to one another within the third degree, if their fathers have exchanged work and feasts over many years. Such children are supposed not eligible as marriage partners under penalties applied for incest. A ritual fine serves in practice to cut the special relationship built up through *megita* activities. Three of nine marriages in Sensuron in 1959–1960 involved ritual payment of a fine to the village headman to cut *megita* ties of the couple's parents. There are 12 *megita* in the 5 territorial divisions of Sensuron.

A third social group with a territorial base is an association of particular nuclear family households within a *koboginan.* These associations, termed *timbaN,* are comprised of nuclear family households considering themselves as neighbors. There were 21 such groups in the 5 Sensuron *koboginan* in 1959–1960, with a range of 3 to 12 nuclear family households. No special names are used to distinguish *timbaN* units. The *timbaN* do not regulate marriage or function in most economic activities. These social groups function as mutual-aid, ceremonial, and political units. In times of crises arising from accident, illness, death, or natural disaster, members are supposed to cooperate in giving help to affected households. Particular ritual acts are conducted by a female specialist especially employed by members to insure protection of the neighborhood from disease givers, spirits of the dead, or unknown agents of harm. In the course of 1959–1960 there were eleven *mENemuhau,* or special rituals, conducted by 9 of the 21 Sensuron *timbaN.* Older men of these groups compose an informal council that may publicly settle disputes arising between members. The basic fighting unit in warfare is comprised of *timbaN* members.

In the mountain areas about Sensuron the nuclear family household resides in an apartment in a structure containing from 10 to 30 other nuclear family households. This building, usually called in English "long house," is marked by its length, a common roof covering all household apartments, and a public veranda along the front of the apartment doors. A typical Dusun long-house village consists of three such structures, each with a particular number of "doors" or apartments, usually with one nuclear family household to each apartment. When sons of such a household marry and there are no empty apartments for the new couple, the custom is to take up residence with the parents of the bridegroom until an apartment is vacant, or a new long house is built when the village is moved closer to lands being cleared for dry rice agriculture.

Sensuron is a "divided long-house" type of community; with a lessening of threats of head-and hand-hunting attacks over the recent years, the nuclear-family-household apartments have come to be separated household dwellings. The process of breaking away from the long-house style of life is advanced enough that Sensuron has the initial appearance of a European village, with separate family structures. But the nuclear-family-household dwellings are lined up with one another in such a fashion that it is possible in Sensuron to sight down a row of dwellings and see clearly the apartments of a long house, nearly identical in construction details and separated by only a few feet on either side from neighbors. Whole sections of the village lack only a common roof to be long houses of 30 or more households.

It should be noted that the Borneo long-house community has often been portrayed as an example of communal or community living evolved by a native people as a means of solving social and economic problems. Rather, the Dusun long house is an association of independent nuclear family households, each recognizable and functioning as the basic social, educational, economic, and political unit.

Descent Groups

In addition to social groups based on territorial associations there is in Sensuron a specific social group (*senAkAgun*) which is derived from recognition by village members that each is a descendant of a particular ancestor whose activities are told in legend and folktale on special occasions of feasting and in whose name land is owned and special rituals are conducted. This group is an ancestor-oriented social entity that depends on links of relationship to the common ancestor in each generation which is acquired through either parent, and not through relationship established to one particular "ego," or person. Such a group is known in anthropology as an *ambilineal descent group.* In Sensuron all village members belong to the same descent group, whose special name is *tohau.* The precise technical term used to describe this type of ambilineal descent group is *maximal ramage,* or *sept.* In 43 communities located on and about the Tambunan plain there was agreement on 7 traditional ancestor-oriented descent group names, while scapegoating stories produced a listing of 6 other supposed ambilineal descent groups, with uncertainty about their existence and location as definable social groups.

On the Tambunan plain 28 of 36 villages claimed descent from the ancestor termed *tohau.* Another 7 villages claimed common descent from an ancestor termed *tAgas.* One village claimed descent from an ancestor known as *tibabar.* In folktales and legends of the creation times various explanations are given for the variety of ancestors and their different names. Typically, the tales involve the description of a migration of an ancestor from a special tree, known as *nunuk ArAgAN,* supposedly located at the confluence of the Labuk and Kegibangan rivers, some 70 miles northeast of Sensuron.

In the Tambunan area the descent groups regulate marriage through insistence on practice of endogamy, or marriage within *senAkAgun.* In Sensuron, in the most recent generation of marriages, 38 of 41 marriages were to persons of the *tohau* group. In the second ascending generation of marriages 18 of 20 were to other *tohau* group members. In the third ascending generation all marriages in 9 instances were within the *tohau* descent group. If a person wishes to marry outside of the *senAkAgun,* a special "cooling" fine of pigs and valuable jars must be exchanged between leaders of the groups involved, a ritual act held to balance social and nonhuman forces brought into opposition by the marriage. After such a marriage the bride lives in the village of the groom, following a rule of residence in marriage termed virilocal, or patrilocal, in comparative studies of human social behavior.

The ambilineal descent group in Sensuron, with others of the Tambunan area, practices common ownership, or *sAgeAn,* of particular types of property in the form of land, fruit, trees, jars, gongs, weapons, and ritual specialist paraphernalia. All members of the descent group have rights of use of these items of property without impairing their value or substance, a practice termed usually as *usufruct* property rights. Moveable items such as gongs and jars are held in trust for all members of the *senAkAgun* by a recognized leader of each ambilineal descent group.

All *senAkAgun* groups are referred to in conversation by use of the special term *sumpuru.* A large jungle tree with many branches emerging high on the trunk is designated by the term *sumpuru.* At times when several "ramage" groups gather for councils of war or to conduct ritual celebrating their alliances in past wars, ceremonial drinking is conducted from a special vessel made of seven small bamboo cups, each hanging from a short piece of rattan, and the whole knotted at the ends of the vines. The cups are symbolic of the supposed seven original ancestors, while the knotted rattans shows the common heritage of all men.

Today in Sensuron neither rice lands nor their irrigation systems are held in common by the "ramage" group. Such property is considered to be similar to gongs, jars, beads, and so forth, and are the corporate possession of the nuclear family household, to be inherited through rules governing all items of property. However, in the mountains about Sensuron land cannot be considered as property of any household, nor can it be inherited by individuals as if it were personal property. Here, rights to lands in all instances are retained by the ramage groups.

Apparently the practice of descent group ownership of land became too cumbersome in Sensuron as new groups settled in the village. With surpluses of food and reduced warfare the population expanded to the point where excess lands for irrigated rice agriculture was no longer available. The corporate rights in land possession apparently shifted from the descent group to the nuclear family households; the household in Sensuron now exercises all rights to rice lands, their improvement and disposal. Under conditions of dry-rice agriculture any land cleared and used by a household was understood to remain the property of the descent group. Few disputes arise over land in hill rice cultivation due to the great unused jungle tracts available for clearing. However, in Sensuron, disputes concerning land are frequent. In records of land ownership registered with the British district officer in Tamunan between 1917 and 1960, 76 of 85 plots of rice lands claimed by Sensuron people were involved in 105 disputes of possession and succession to the land.

However, the descent group still controls land tenure for most areas in the hills about the village according to traditional rights of use. Land used for gardens and areas planted for cash crops are still considered under control of the ramage.

The leader, or headman, of a *senAkAgun* group is selected in each generation through vigorous public discussion and general consent of group members.

A new ramage headman may be the son of a deceased leader, but the rights of leadership are not hereditary.

The descent group leader is chosen partly for his power of *mEgEndAr-Ase,* or "ability to frighten" disputing members of the group into agreement. This power, supposedly transmitted from the creators to the common ancestor and then on to the descent group leader of each generation, is the force the creators use to threaten persons disturbing the peace of society. The descent group leader is reputed, in the words of *MarkosIn* of Sensuron, "to be so smart that when he talks people are afraid of him." The selection process of a ramage leader is said to be final when the headman of each village of the descent group, themselves said possessed of some *mEgEndArAse* power, come together in a council to agree on the new leader of the descent group. The descent group leader takes precedence over village headmen in all matters of ritual, ceremony, or adjudication of disputes. Large-scale efforts of a political and economic nature are directed by the descent group headman. Disputes between members are usually heard and judged by the descent group leader in council, with the headmen of villages of disputants. Such meetings are public and involve special tests of truth and oaths (see Chapter 7) and particular punishments, ranging from fines to ostracism or death by beating or stoning.

Tambunan descent group differences are marked today through dialect, food habits, certain behavior forms, and styles of gong and vocal music.

Kindred Groups

A second social group based on recognition of descent is found in Sensuron and in the Tambunan area villages. This group, termed a *bilateral kindred* in comparative studies of social behavior, is composed of persons recognizing their relationships to a particular individual, without regard to whether the relationship is through a male or female relative. Thus, from the point of view of a particular individual in Sensuron, membership in this social group (*tengran*) is comprised ideally of that group of living relatives from great grandparents through seventh cousins in the father's line of descent and from great grandparents to third cousins in the mother's line of descent, with inclusion of all affinals, or persons married to relatives in this range.

In contemporary village life the bilateral kindred is restricted usually to all living descendents, and their spouses, of the eight great grandparents, thus extending the group laterally to include only third cousins in both the father's and mother's line of descent. In daily affairs individuals in Sensuron may have little social contact with all members of even this more restricted group of persons, yet the accounting of kindred members is of prime social significance. This group defines the practical range of bilateral kindred exogamy, or the social limits beyond which a marriage partner must be chosen, and is the village social unit of most importance beyond the nuclear family household. Under severe penalties of incest marriage must take place outside the real *tengran.* In Sensuron, of 70 marriages in the three most recent generations there were none within the third degree of relationship.

From the point of reference of the Sensuron individual the *tengran* is seen as a series of ever-widening social groupings branching out through the father's and mother's personal bilateral kindreds.

The father's personal *tengran* and the mother's *tengran* are the most immediate group of persons to be recognized and dealt with as kindred. The important link between these two different kindred groups is the affinal, or marriage, relationship between parents of the individual. In turn it is the affinal relationship that links the *tengran* of the father's father and father's mother and the mother's father and mother's mother. In the first three ascending generations all affinally linked bilateral kindreds are counted to make up a large group of relatives, formally termed either *matu,* or *tapinai dE yahai* ("all persons of my kindred"). Persons descended from ancestors beyond the third ascending generation of kindred are recognized by use of the term *menembali.* The general term *tapinai* ("relative") is used in Sensuron to designate the limits of socially recognized bilateral kindred relationships; if a person is *tapinai,* they are to be included as part of the *tengran* group. Special friends may be incorporated into the group of *tapinai* and thus become kindred members.

Two identical rituals are held sometime after the thirtieth day of birth and these are intended as formal presentation of the child to the father's father and mother's father as representatives of the four kindreds in the second ascending generation and, in turn, the kindreds of each earlier generation, each linked through marriage.

Marriage and Divorce

No other social relationship in Sensuron has the importance of marriage, because of the emphasis placed upon this relationship in the definition of the bilateral kindred. Hence marriage is seen as too important an event to be left entirely to the desires of younger and less experienced persons. Although a boy or girl, having reached the age of sexual maturity and exhibiting the possession of character expected for young men and young women, have a choice of marriage partners within the limits of the incest rules, all formal arrangements for marriage are initiated by the groom's father, paternal grandfather, a father's brother, or one of father's or grandfather's special friends. It is usually the boy who initiates a request of his father to make marriage arrangements, after having made a secret agreement with the girl about their marriage.

Marriage always involves direct and substantial property payment, or *nApAN,* by the groom to the father of the bride. This payment of gongs, jars, and animals is not intended as a "price" for the bride, but is supposed to "represent" her in the nuclear family household by "staying in her place" to comfort her parents in her absence. Traditionally, no less *nApAN* can be given than a girl's mother claims her father received. Arguments between the parents of the boy and the girl often develop over the accuracy of the claims of the bride's mother regarding the value of *nApAN* paid to her father.

At the time *nApAN* is paid, a token payment, termed *tEtub* ("to keep company") is made also by the groom to the bride's father as a piece of property to accompany the *nApAN* items and to "comfort" these items that are absent from their familiar places in the boy's household. The bride makes a token payment to the groom's father equal in value to that of the *tEtub,* as a "small return" in recognition of payment of the *nApAN.*

The arrangements of marriage, begun by representatives of the boy, are conducted formally and by the reputedly most sober representatives that can be selected; it is considered fair to get the boy's representative in marriage arrangements drunk and have him agree to a much higher *nApAN* than otherwise would be paid.

The wedding is a daylong feast intended to ally the bilateral kindreds of the couple through formal sharing of food and drink. When the feasting is over at sundown the girl retires with the boy for the night in a sleeping area of his house. The initial acts of intercourse at the boy's house are called *metAllmbAgu* ("exchanging newness"), and are repeated the next night at the girl's house after a second day of feasting, where the boy is "new to the girl's family."

After the wedding events, the couple usually establishes first residence with the boy's parents until or shortly after birth of their first child. Then the couple must move into a nuclear family household of their own.

Initial residence at marriage in Sensuron was established virilocally, or with the boy's father, in 61 of 70 marriages in the three most recent generations. In 6 of the 70 marriages the couple established initial residence with the bride's parents. Such preference, termed uxorilocal, occurs when the bride has no brothers and she has aged or ill parents with substantial wealth to manage. Initial residence in 3 of 70 marriages was with the bride's parents, and then the couple moved to residence with the groom's parents.

The prevailing or regular residence rule in Sensuron marriage is, however, an ambilocal type, that is, the married couple take up permanent residence in a house structure located apart, yet near both their nuclear family households.

Marriages in Sensuron are usually monogamous. Second wives may be taken, but only if chosen with specific regard to the ideal rules for descent group endogamy, bilateral kindred exogamy, and with full payment of property as *nApAN* and *tEtub.* Then the circumstances of the proposed plural marriage must be discussed within the kindred and descent groups to determine whether the parties involved are to be permitted this form of social behavior. Payment of full *nApAN* in a second marriage is exceedingly expensive, usually three times the ordinary amount, because of the demands of the girls' father who knows his daughter is to be a secondary wife. Therefore most men cannot afford more than one wife. Secondary wives are treated as junior household members by both the husband and the first wife. There were four households in Sensuron in 1959–1960 that contained secondary wives; in two of the four there was one additional wife, acquired by payment of *nApAN* and from the ideal ranges of incest exogamy. In the remaining two households the secondary wives each had been sisters-in-law, taken in marriage by a man after the death of a younger brother. This practice, termed the levirate, is said in Sensuron to be a means of insuring that the woman and her dependent children remain the responsibility of her late husband's kindred.

Termination of any marriage, other than through death, must involve return of property paid to the person judged at fault in separation. A ritual fine may be requested in addition to "cool" the anger of the creator at a disturbance of the marriage relationship. Reasons for divorce in Sensuron are said to be: (1) a failure of a woman to bear children, (2) an "unkind" (cruel) husband or wife, (3) lack of work by either partner, (4) lack of work skills required of a spouse, (5) adultery, and (6) desertion. Disagreements between marriage partners are first discussed in the presence of the parents, or representatives of the parents, and then are taken to the village headman for a full hearing of claims and counterclaims. The initial hearing by a headman is an effort to prevent a divorce. The headman seeks to arbitrate, with the help of the couple's parents, to avoid breaking off bilateral kindred ties established by the marriage. If the initial hearing of the matter fails to produce agreement by the couple, then a formal, public hearing of divorce is held to establish fault and to determine the types and amounts of property to be returned. Each instance of action for divorce has definitions of fault, value to be repaid, and fines to be levied against the offending party. Divorce is recognized as final when the repayment of property and fines are settled, and the offended spouse formally says, in the presence of the headman and both sets of parents, *yAdaun ku*! ("I desert her"), or *nAdA oku*! ("I leave him!"). In Sensuron approximately 10 percent of all marriages end in divorce, while another 10 percent, particularly those among childless and newly married couples, are in states of chronic conflict that may be settled eventually by divorce. Wife beatings and brawls between spouses enliven many days. A frequent reason for arguments between spouses and divorce which is unstated generally or covered over with other causes, is the bullying of the bride by her mother-in-law. Since the girl must work for some time under the direction of her mother-in-law, clashes are frequent on questions of procedure, skill, and attitudes to work. In seven Sensuron marriages in 1959–1960 brides left their husbands in anger for periods of a week to three months. In three of the seven instances a dominant mother-in-law was said to be responsible.

Kinship Terminology

Social relations within the bilateral kindred, descent group, and in territorially based groups are established and maintained generally through use of special kin terms. These terms carry meanings in such social groups for both the speakers and hearers, and are weighted with a great amount of emotion for their users.

Thus kinship terms in Sensuron are basic to a system of meanings and associated behavior patterns that define expected rights, duties, and concerns of the individual in day-to-day and special social situations.

Kinship terms used for talking about (reference terms) consanguineal relatives, that is, persons said related by a common heredity, separate the nuclear family (father, mother, son, daughter) from all relatives not considered in the line of descent, or all collateral relatives. Collateral relatives are not distinguished from each other in reference terms. There is a limited use of terms for talking about brothers and sisters, with distinctions used in such terms that are based on age and sex of the person discussed. Terms used for talking about cousins are of the "Eskimo type," that is, "cross-cousins" (the children of a man and his sister) and "parallel-cousins" (the children of two brothers or two sisters) are called by the same terms, but are terminologically distinguished from siblings.[1]

There is a special use of kin terms for dicusssing a relative through marriage, such as a sister-in-law or a brother-in-law.

The terms used for direct address (vocative terms) also form a special group. In direct address parents are distinguished from their brothers, sisters and cousins. Brothers and sisters of the speaker are called by terms that distinguish age and sex of the person addressed, and cousins are addressed through use of terms that designate the precise degree of relationship to the speaker. Nieces and nephews and children of all cousins are addressed by a term that is taken from one used in speaking to father's brothers and mother's brothers.

There are differences in using kin terms to talk about or address different generations. In the grandparent generation, the general reference term of grandparent is used for all brothers, sisters, cousins, and spouses of the grandparents in both lines. The sex of grandparents is distinguished by terms for grandfather and grandmother. All persons beyond the grandparents generation are referred to by a special kin term. In the parent's generation, mother and father are distinguished from their same sex siblings; father's brother and mother's brother are designated as "uncle," and mother's sister and father's sister are termed, "aunt." In direct address to these relatives mother's and father's brothers are distinguished by special terms, as are mother's and father's sisters. These differentiations in terms of address are used also for cousins of mother and father, and the spouses of parent's cousins.

In the same generation as the speaker, kinship terms have more variety of form. There are several general terms for talking about brothers and sisters, and there are general terms to refer to all brothers, or all sisters, of the speaker. And there are specific terms for talking about one brother or one sister. Sex and age distinctions of brothers and sisters can also be noted by use of particular terms. Terms used for cousins indicate the precise degree or range of relationship to

---

[1] In studying the ways different peoples classify their social relationships, anthropologists have found certain regularities of kinship terminology. Terms for cousins, as they are related to those for brothers, sisters, uncles, and nephews, have been chosen as a basis for establishing models for studies of kin terms. Names of peoples who typically have these types of kin terms have been given to these models. Thus, the models for study of kinship terminology are called Eskimo, Hawaiian, Iroquois, Sudanese, Omaha, Crow, Dakota, Fox, Guinea, Nankanse, and Yuman. For a discussion of these models, see George P. Murdock, *Social Structure*. New York: Macmillan, 1949.

the speaker. A general term is used to refer to cousins of either sex in either line of descent to any degree of relationship.

In the first generation younger than the speaker, terms for talking about children are confined to the speaker's own offspring or descendents. Sex of the child is referred to by a special term. Terms of address for children also reflect distinctions based on sex. The children of the speaker's brothers and sisters are spoken about through use of the same term used to address father's and mother's brothers. The general term for grandchild is applied to all descendents and spouses of descendents in the second generation younger than the speaker.

Terms used for talking about relatives by marriage include special uses for such persons as parent-in-law, child-in-law, wife's sister, husband's sister, brother's wife, wife's brother's wife, and so on. Husbands and wives are referred to by special terms. Relatives by marriage can be referred to and addressed by kin terms used for consanguineal relatives if social relations are in the same generation and are close. Such relations and kin uses are not possible between a speaker and relatives by marriage in the next older generation because the pattern of avoidance of a parent-in-law is generalized to all relatives of this age and class.

In addition to these kin terms, used primarily within the bilateral kindred group, there are a number of collective terms used to include other persons (for example, *megita* or *timbaN* members), considered as kindred members.

Kinship Terms and Social Roles

Kin terms refer not only to biological relationships but also the the social facts of role behavior expectations. The most important fact about a kinship system is that it is a series of role behavior indicators that make it possible for an individual to know what to expect from his kin and to understand what kinsmen expect of him.

Relationships between social roles and kin terms are best seen in operation in the Sensuron nuclear family household. The nuclear family is organized about the fact of a father's authority over his children and wife. A father is believed ideally to be a person whose power to make decisions and act should be unquestioned. Relationships between a father and his children, and especially sons, are usually tense and are often broken completely through a child leaving home to take up residence with a grandparent, an uncle or a friend's parents. Dusun patriarchal control in a household may result in an offended or angry child, and occasionally even leads to a form of hysterical behavior (*mEguEd*), in which attacks are made by a child on the symbols of father's authority; the valued personal property of father is broken and thrown out of the house by a child screaming outrage and offense at his father. A Sensuron father indulges behavior by a daughter challenging his authority that would bring a beating to a boy. Usually such toleration of behavior derives from awareness of the fact that girls will live in another household after marriage.

Relationships between mothers and children are less stressed and seem marked by considerable indulgence of challenges to mother's authority and power. This indulgence is partly based upon a Dusun mother's sense of close relationship to a child, and partly because she clearly lacks power to discipline her children effectively without her husband's support. When relationships between parents are strained, as they often are, Sensuron mothers exercise little effective control over children. These patterns of parent-child kin relationships are tempered by role behavior forms of the oldest and youngest sons with parents. Since ideal inheritance patterns tend to provide that the oldest son will acquire most property to be left by parents, his responses to father and mother tend to be shaped by this fact. The youngest son is expected to be the source of support for parents in their old age. Relationships between a father and his youngest son are as close as any entered into by a father with children. The youngest son often becomes the "tattletale" of the children and learns to control his parents with the implicit threat of desertion in their old age.

Sibling role behavior is characterized by rules of seniority in age and by sex. Older children take priority in most instances over younger children, while boys are given the advantage over girls in all instances. Relationships between brothers and sisters are not generally close and are marked by frequent fights and quarrels.

Relationships between spouses seem to be a delicate balance between mutual concern arising from long, close personal association and specific threats of deprivation of personal services. As noted earlier, wives often leave husbands for long periods of time. These are times when a wife is seeking to check or alter husband's authority through depriving him of her personal economic and sexual services. Husbands in turn threaten wives with deprivation of support in subsistence activities and protection. Wife beatings are not unusual in Sensuron. Failing to subdue a wife through threats, husbands often use violence to achieve their ends of personal authority. Beatings may be mutually administered, for not all Dusun women submit quietly to a husband's violence; four times in one year in Sensuron there were spectacular public husband-wife fights in which the wife gave as much as she received from her husband. In many Sensuron households relationships between spouses are quieter and not marked by many quarrels or much personal abuse. But in many of these households lack of argument between spouses is only a state of hostile truce, easily broken at times of drinking, with loud quarrels and charges of adultery and fornication. Sensuron wives often seek sexual relationships outside of marriage so they can threaten to expose an abusive husband in order to ridicule him concerning his "manhood" and virility. Husbands regularly respond to such threats with verbal and physical abuse. Husbands are not able to counter-threaten a wife with announcement of sexual adventures outside of marriage, since it is supposed that a man can engage in intercourse without really harming the character of his marriage relationship.

A Sensuron child learns early that forms of role behavior to be expected of grandparents differ greatly from those of either parent. The authority of a father or mother is regularly altered by a grandfather or grandmother, and indulgences by parents are more than matched by grandparents. Father's father or mother's father provide safe havens for a grandchild fleeing the authority and power of punishment of a father. A grandfather comes to be the referee of parent-child disputes, with the paternal grandfather often exercising his own authority of age over his son on behalf of a grandchild, and a maternal grandfather using his authority of the parent-in-law avoidance pattern toward the father.

Role behavior relationships between an individual and his relatives by marriage are marked by generally different expectations and responsibilities than those obtaining with consanguineal kin. Since marriage is seen as an alliance between kin groups, parents-in-law are considered as representatives of the authority and power of the wife's total bilateral kindred and are usually treated with deference and respect that takes the form of avoidance of all unnecessary conversation or mention by name. This pattern is supposed to be strongest for relationships with the spouse's parent of the opposite sex; a Sensuron husband avoids his wife's mother as much as possible, rarely speaks to or of her, and only indicates his tensions concerning her through mild jokes. A Sensuron wife, as indicated earlier, usually begins married life in the household of her husband and thus is thrown into constant daily contacts with her husband's mother. The ideals of deference, respect, and avoidance for a daughter-in-law and mother-in-law relationship are placed in jeopardy by such contacts because of the necessity for cooperative work at household tasks.

Role behavior relations between individuals and the brothers and sisters of a spouse are restrained. While such relationships are not marked by patterns of avoidance and deference accorded to parents-in-law, it is only on rare occasions that a brother or sister-in-law, are considered personally close enough to give confidences to or provide advice on action.

Forms of role behavior common between the brothers or sisters of a parent toward a child, and for a child to such persons, are marked by patterns similar to those existing between grandparents and grandchildren. A father's brother is usually the next person after grandfathers that a child turns to for help in tempering his father's uses of authority. Father's brothers, especially younger ones, tend to even the scores of childhood arguments by standing up for a nephew or niece in their challenge to parental powers. A father's sister is a teacher of domestic skills and confidant to her young nieces. Her relationships with nephews are marked by sexual joking. The conduct of such a relationship is firmly within the bounds of the incest rules; despite sexual joking relationships between father's sister and nephews, sexual intercourse between them is considered as repugnant as between a mother and son. The brothers and sisters of a mother are considered as being also able to temper parental authority and provide affection.

7

Property, Order, and Authority

MATERIAL POSSESSIONS in Sensuron, are associated with the social system through a set of beliefs that link people to things. These beliefs about relationships between persons and objects make up a form of a property system, that is, a collection of ideas concerning all types of ownership of property, and all means of acquisition, exchange, or disposal of property. Since many social relationships in which property is involved are nonkinship relations and not directed by rules of kinship behavior, there is a formal series of rights, duties, privileges, and powers for ordering the links between people and things. When people disagree in social relations or concerning property, the problems are solved generally through appeal to the authority of the neighborhood, village, or descent group councils to bring power to bear in the issue to force proper behavior.

Property

The people of Sensuron treat things as being either movable or immovable in nature. There are ten classes of movable property and two classes of immovable property. All property, or *nauetAn* (or *nietAn*), is felt to be possessed of a personal history, beginning with a "birth" in manufacture or in natural events, through a "life" of unique experiences, to a "death" by human sale, consumption, or destruction. The ten classes of movable property are: (1) *tAk-Anan,* all stored food stuffs, such as rice; (2) *dapo,* or gongs, jars, tools, and weapons; (3) *tiam,* all animals of the groups of pigs, fowl, and *kerabau*; (4) *kenitAn,* all property brought by a wife to her marriage, which may include any of the classes of movable and immovable property; (5) *narAnki-gEndIN-kambarANun,* objects used in ceremonial activities; (6) *tealus,* property acquired as payment for ceremonial services; (7) *tEnkosAn,* property inherited from the bilateral kin group; (8) *nIndEpuAn,* property acquired through personal labor; (9) *basAn dE tandu,* female property such as clothing, rings, and beads, and (10) *nApAN,* property acquired in marriage of a daughter.

The two classes of immovable property are land *lagit* or *pEtebAsAn*) and houses (*uali* or *lAmIn*). Together the 12 classes of property comprise the limits of personal property, *antEb dE dogo* ("everything of mine"). Property is said to be acquired through one of six means: (1) trade, (2) inheritance, (3) manufacture, (4) agriculture and gardening, (5) gathering, or (6) marriage. All forceful acquisition of property is regarded as theft, unless the act occurs during the special circumstances of a war raid. Such property is considered part of an individual's *narAnki-gEndIN-kambarANun* class of possessions.

The ownership of an item of property can never be in doubt if paid for properly, and witnessed by one other person. Aquisition of property in proper form gives the right to dispose of the object or land through sale or gift under the rule that "what is bought is mine to do as I will."

Parents regularly tell children detailed stories concerning the manner in which property was acquired or disposed of so they will know "how to acquire and want more property" and the precise value of their potential inheritance. It is believed the prime good of property is that it serves as protection from want in old age and improves the good name of the household.

Property can be disposed of through deliberate destruction as the consequence of anger. It is believed that great anger, or offense, is demonstrated through public abandonment or destruction of valued goods. In late 1959 a 67-year-old male of Sensuron became angry at a judgment that was brought against him in a land dispute. He returned from the hearing, got drunk and proceeded to destroy his house by cutting the rattan ties that held the bamboo sections to the house frame. These sections were thrown away from the house, sailing off into a large crowd of spectators, where they were picked up and carried off by a number of persons. At the end of three hours of drinking, of screaming curses at the village council and of cutting at rattan ties, the old man had stripped the bamboo walls, floor, and roof away from the house frame. Then he cut or uprooted the house frame and finally left to sleep in his rice storehouse. The next day, sober, he tried to get the bamboo and posts returned to him. In most instances he was refused the materials. In a later village council hearing it was judged he had relinquished all rights to this property by throwing it away and could not reclaim it.

Women engage in destruction of property as often as men. In 1959–1960 there were six instances of males and five instances of females engaging in acts of public destruction of personal property. There is no restriction on an adult woman acquiring or disposing of property. Women who acquire and hold large amounts of personal property do so through both inheritance and profits of work, exchange of foodstuffs, or sale of items manufactured for personal wear, and through the making of domestic tools, which are reinvested in *kerabou,* gongs, jars, or land.

Inheritance of property in the class of *tEnkosAn,* which includes usually all personal property in the classes of *dapo, tiam, nIndEpuAn,* and *nApAN,* follows a well-defined set of rules. When a father dies his sons, and ideally the oldest son, are his heirs. If the sons are dead and there are grandsons, they jointly become heirs. If a man had no sons, his *tEnkosAn* goes to his daughters, and ideally the oldest daughter. If the daughters are deceased, but there are sons, the property is paid to them equally, or, if there are no daughter's sons, the property goes to daughter's daughters. If there are no heirs in this group, a condition known as *INgA tEmunkus* ("none to inherit") is applied. The rule of inheritance is that heirs must be "sought out" by the property, or *mEgeum dE id sAmEk* ("it goes looking for someone") in the wider circle of bilateral kin. If a man dies without children, the *tEnkosAn* is usually paid to his oldest brother, or sometimes to all brothers, and, if there are no brothers alive, to their sons. If the brother had no sons, the *tEnkosAn* is paid to brother's daughters. If there are no heirs in this group, the property is paid to the sisters of the deceased. If the sisters are deceased, the property is paid to the sisters' sons or a sister's son's sons. When all of these classes of kin are exhausted in the search for heirs, the property will revert to the deceased male's father's brothers, or sisters and their heirs.

The pattern of heirship in *tEnkosAn* can be altered by the specific bequests of a father. It is not unusual for a father to publicly disinherit a particular son or daughter by a statement in the form of: "If you inherit my property, I will curse you!"

Long-lasting arguments between sons and daughters are frequent on the matter of intent of a dead father regarding inheritance of *tEnkosAn.* A father's decisions regarding distribution of his property among his children ideally depends upon "the way a child behaves." Sensuron fathers often warn sons or daughters challenging their authority through use of the phrase *kAdA kous!* or "do not take offense!" meaning in full, "do not take offense when I leave you no property!" Such a threat is responded to usually by submission of a child to his father's wishes, since disinheritance is both a matter of deprivation of wealth and public disgrace.

While property in the classes of *nIndapuAn* and *nApAN* are considered part of *tEnkosAn,* there are special rules for their disposal. Although a husband and wife have labored together to acquire property, it is usually considered to be owned by the male. However, when he dies, the wife can expect her son or sons, or daughters, to "remember" her interest in the *nIndApuAn* and to support her from its earnings and to give her at least half the proceeds from any sale of such property. If there are no children, any of the deceased male's *nIndapuAn* acquired through mutual efforts with his wife is split equally between his brothers or sisters and wife. The same rules may apply to disposal of *nApAN.*

Property owned by a woman at her death, such as *kenitan, nIndapuAn, basAn dE tandu,* and so on, is distributed to her children, usually in equal shares. If there are no children, her property is paid to her brothers, or if her brothers are deceased, to brother's sons, or daughters if there are no sons. If there are no brothers, such property is inherited by her sisters or their sons and daughters.

On the occasions when a father dies leaving young children, inheritance of property is suspended until they become adults and a guardian is charged with responsibility for the property. Usually a guardian is a husband's brother, or if he has no brothers, one of his sisters. When a wife cares for her children in her nuclear family household, a guardian will not physically hold possession of property, and there is no fee paid him for advice or help in his trust functions. If the guardianship involves care of orphaned children, or the presence of the widow and family in the husband's brother's nuclear family household, the guardianship for property is known as foster parenthood, and a small fee is allowed the guardian for his custodianship of property. The responsibility of a guardian is to care for the property to see that it remains undiminished in value until paid to the heirs.

Although inheritance of land and houses follows the usual rule for distribution of property to heirs, there is often dispute concerning particular parcels of land or a special structure. A common saying in the village reflects an intensity of feeling concerning land, "I would rather live without jars and gongs than to be without land to till!"

While distribution of property after death may conform to the usual rules of inheritance, it does not always follow that there will not be an attempt by some heir to raise a question concerning payment of land; of the 105 land disputes noted in the previous chapter, 41 concerned inheritance and were challenges by an heir who felt that the distribution of land was improper. Such disputes reflect the transition from descent group ownership of land to individual inheritance; land, as an item of property, was not included in the *tEnkosAn, nIndapuAn,* or *nApAN* until the past two generations. Now, with new land in Sensuron no longer readily available for wet-rice cultivation, challenges are made concerning the traditional rules of inheritance of property in attempts to secure a base of personal wealth and economic security.

Beliefs concerning the borrowing and lending of property involve a set of ideas concerning rights and duties of property. If a person owes another a debt of property, but refuses to pay, the person owed can claim his rights through a formal hearing before the village council. Since no symbols of debts are used in Sensuron, all notations of debt owed and paid are kept through use of witnesses. Repayment of property borrowed usually involves the public statement, "Look here, I repay the goods I have owed to you." The class of property most commonly involved in borrowing is *tAkAnan,* or stored food, especially rice. There are 15 households of 183 in Sensuron that regularly borrow rice to eat in the period just prior to the annual harvest. And in times when the rice crop has failed through a natural disaster the borrowing of food to stave off famine is common. If one carrying-basket of rice is borrowed, then interest in the form of one quarter of a basket is charged with repayment at the next harvest. If the loan is not repaid at the next harvest, the interest on the loan is computed to repayment of the one basket borrowed, plus one-half basket for missing payment at the first harvest. If a third harvest goes by without payment of the loan, the amount owed becomes one basket for the original loan, one-half basket for interest on the second harvest after the loan, and one-half basket for interest for the third harvest after the loan. Failure to repay the loan after a third harvest often results in the lender requesting a hearing to judge default on the loan.

A debt is considered to never expire; a saying notes that a man's debts, like the roots of the fallen jungle softwood tree, continue to grow after his death. So to prevent accumulation of interest payments, debts of a deceased person are paid relatively soon after his death.

In most Sensuron households, however, there are several property debts outstanding. In one household a series of debts had grown over three generations to at least 28 specific obligations, ranging in value from one-half basket of rice to five grown male *kerabou.* Since children and grandchildren become responsible for the debts of parents and grandparents, obligations can be assumed by a young man that were incurred at another time. Of the total of 28 debts, 18 were those owed by the father, father's brothers, and father's father.

Order and Authority

Every human group must develop means of using force, power, and authority within the territory it occupies. In Sensuron there are two means of controlling and using force, power, and authority—traditional law and war. Traditional law consists of a set of ideas concerning peaceful settlement of disputes and making of decisions. War is the form used to make others comply with decisions or settlements of disagreements. Social force, power, or authority exist in any social relationship when one person can make others do as he wants them to do either through law or war.

Social power is derived in Sensuron, from age, sex, property, personal knowledge, and reputation for adherence to traditional law. All social power rests upon particular conceptions of truth and justice. For Dusun "justice is as a stone rolling down the mountain, for as the stone has no eyes, so justice is blind and beats down error." Truth is believed a definable essence of the universe, which exists always, without change, and can be determined through special ritual tests in administration of justice. Truth is said to be manifest, or visible, in traditional law. Wrongs or crimes are felt caused by faulty biological heritage that results in flawed personal character, or by social tensions that produce anger and frustration which, in turn, lead to action violating traditional law. In Sensuron a lie is said to be a violation of traditional law that leads to damage to interests of other persons, since it is believed that damage to truth by one person tends to damage the whole community.

Political activity in Sensuron centers upon the persons possessed of the most force for insuring compliance with their wishes; such individuals usually are older men in control of a great amount of property and skilled in male specialities such as hunting, fishing, war, and toolmaking. More importantly, these men are adept at explaining and and recalling details of traditional law. From their knowledge they gain reputations as interpreters of truth and representatives of justice. A village leader exercises his personal power over others not only because he is also a senior male, wealthy in property, skilled in most male activities, and "wise" in his judgments under law, but because he is felt possessed of more of each of these characters than other men of power. And added to these qualities is the authority of *mEgEndArAse,* which, as noted in the previous chapter, is an ability to frighten persons into agreement. Generally a village headman exhibits a tolerance of dispute and a genuine affection for nonrelatives not characteristic of other Dusun. His daily contacts with people of the village are mostly cheerful and often intimate, and of the order of a father with a favorite child. A village leader may direct a burial party, supervise digging of an irrigation channel, decide on the time for a ritual, interpret a dream, advise on proper knots for tying a house together, or test out a new musical instrument. At the outset of their terms as political leaders, headmen tend to exhibit the ideal personality characteristics expected of a political leader. As their powers become tested through passage of time, they may appeal to the tradition of their leadership. Some headmen become less inclined to truth in their relationships with others as a means of forcing others to comply with their decisions. As the headman shows he will lie to serve his personal ambitions, fear of his supernatural powers diminishes and respect for his judgments of truth and justice lessens. In several villages near Sensuron the headman was so little respected that he was powerless in most social situations. Dusun are firm in their insistence that a liar cannot interpret truth.

A headman or *timbaN* leader that does not live up to ideal expectations of him will have his powers limited through gossip about him, be ignored openly, or even told to mind his business. In such instances power shifts to one or several other persons possessed of ideal qualities of leadership, and the power structure and uses of the community continue to operate, although indirectly, until the headman dies or retires. There is no procedure for recalling a headman.

A descent group leader is expected to meet fully the ideals of character and behavior described above, and usually does. There appear to be some descent group leaders with a tendency to stinginess, lying, and exploitation, but most are men demonstrating power through personal character that leave little doubt concerning their status. Relations between village leaders who make up the council of the descent group, and the descent group headman depend very much on the reputation of the village leader for truth, generosity, and lack of exploitation.

The system of traditional law in use in Sensuron operates simply: the norms ("manners," "ethics," "morals") of Dusun law are known to exist as given from the time of creation and the ancestors, and are provided authority through use over generations. Norms are felt never to change. When an individual breaks a norm through a social act that is unacceptable according to definition of the norm, then action is taken on the matter before a village headman or council, or a descent group headman or council. Anyone injured by a violation of a norm is expected to seek the advice of the village headman, and so begin proceedings to judge the merit of his claim and possible compensation for damages to person or property. A person feeling wronged by another generally forfeits his right to appeal through a hearing if he commits another offense in return.

In Dusun traditional law 58 separate offenses are grouped into 6 general classifications of: (1) offenses against the person, (2) sex and marriage offenses,

(3) property offenses, (4) fraud, (5) social offenses, and (6) religious offenses. Sanctions generally are concerned with secular matters, rather than religious offenses; only 6 of 58 offenses are concerned with religious behavior. The greatest number of offenses in one class are those concerning definitions of acts of physical and verbal aggression against others.

Sanctions levied for the various classes of offenses are of four types: (1) death, either through beating or stoning, (2) banishment from the community, (3) fines in property, and (4) ritual payment (*sAgIt*), to "cool off" heat of the universe caused by an offense. Each type of sanction may be applied to most offenses. The punishment of death can be applied in all classes of offense except social offenses and fraud. The sanction of expulsion from the village is used in all offense classes except fraud. The sanctions of property fines and ritual payments are applied in all classes of offense. Application of punishments follows a series of definitions of grades of severity of an offense. A sanction is usually applied depending on whether the offense is the first, second, third, or fourth accusation of the same person for the same violation of traditional law. Sanctions are applied according to a complex scale of worth of persons and property.

As noted, an appeal to the village headman or council for redress of a wrong begins the formal determination of whether an offense has been committed, and whether sanctions need be applied to preserve the integrity of traditional law. When a report of an offense is made to the headman, the complainant is advised publicly not to compound the offense through any actions that would be offenses. The warning takes the report from the status of a private dispute to that of a matter of public concern. If a complaint involves a minor offense, and there is no similar complaint and judgment against the person supposed to have committed the offense, the headman settles the matter through an informal meeting of the persons involved. Such informal adjudication is usually held in the headman's yard and ends with him advising everyone concerned to forget the matter. When the headman considers an offense to be of a major type, he arranges for a formal hearing before the village council. At a time chosen by the headman the council assembles before the headman's house, usually arranging itself by sitting in a semicircle, facing the accused, complainant, and witnesses for each side. Hearings of major offenses are attended by most persons in a community, who cluster behind the witnesses, facing the headman and council members.

In major offenses such as incest, adultery, cursing to death, and murder, both the accused and the complainant are required publicly to swear a sacred oath to establish their rights to justice. The oath notes:

> I cut this grass with my fingernail; this grass is as my heart's artery. If I tell the truth, your heart's artery will be cut as I cut this grass. If I lie, my heart's artery will be cut as I have cut this grass.

Once the oath has been taken the complainant presents his case, first by relating his grievance, then through presenting witnesses in support of his contentions.

Witnesses are required to take an oath before the headman; knotting a piece of rattan about the neck of a witness, the headman says:

Look up disease givers and souls of the dead, there in the earth!
Look, all you spirits of harm!
If this one tells lies, his throat will be cut, as I cut this rattan!

Slicing through the rattan, the headman bids the witness to speak the truth before the creators. In court tests and hearings the creators are invoked in a manner that characterizes them as an avenger force protecting truth.

There can be no hearing for any major offense without witnesses to support all parties to a dispute. And no hearing can be held without initiation of a complaint of wrong by an aggrieved person. There appears to be no means in traditional law for the community to take action through initiation of a complaint by the village headman.

When the complainant finishes his statement and has supported his account with witnesses, the accused is given an opportunity to fully relate his version of events and to have his witnesses give support to his account. Then the council questions both parties and witnesses, in any order and on any question raised in any statement made by all parties to the hearing. After there are no more questions on details of events, the council debates issues involved and weighs them against their knowledge of traditional law. It is ofter necessary for these deliberations to be interrupted for administration of one of several special tests of truth to the complainant and the accused. A ritual specialist, either male or female, administers a lengthy special oath to both parties before they are subjected to a test to determine which one "holds to the truth." The most commonly used tests are: (1) *petAlAdun,* or "a cutting test," (2) *metAlAp,* "a water test," and (3) *metuge,* or "the boiling water test." In *petAlAdun* the accused and the complainant place their right index fingers side by side and a ritual specialist chops down at the tips with the headman's knife; it is believed the innocent will not move or be cut, for they are protected by the truth. In *metAp* both parties go to the nearest river and at a signal from the ritual specialist, immerse themselves totally in the water; it is believed that the party not telling the truth "cannot stay below the water, "for his lies bloat his belly," and so bouy him up. In *metuge* the accused and the complainant must together plunge their right hands into a pot of boiling water held by a ritual specialist; it is supposed a person telling the truth will not be harmed. Such special tests of truth are used only when the council cannot establish the nature of truth in the comments of complainants, accused, and supporting witnesses.

In cases where the council or headman reach a judgment without use of tests of truth, the penalty to be applied is announced publicly. If no penalty is announced, there can be no assumption of conviction in the hearing.

When the offense is one for which death or banishment are possible penalties, or in which a life has been taken, the hearing may move to the home of the descent group leader, where the case is judged by the council members of the descent group through use of the general procedures described above.

Justice in Sensuron is considered done when an offense under traditional law has been "made straight" through a properly conducted hearing, judgment, and payment of penalties. One of the highest compliments to be paid another in the village is to say, "that man gives justice to all."

In the course of a year in Sensuron the headman informally heard 13 minor complaints and conducted 16 formal hearings. In 9 of the formal hearings before the council the matters involved 2 disputes over inheritance, 2 concerning animal ownership, 1 dispute over marriage payments, and 4 cases involving land ownership and water rights for irrigation. The other 7 formal hearings involved traditional law offenses of striking with the fist, threatening with words, cheating on commonly owned property, adultry, jealousy, theft, and drunkeness. The hearings for offenses of traditional law such as adultery, jealousy, and theft were concluded with fines in property and ritual payments. The remainder were settled through restitution of damages and a property fine. The formal hearings were all held before the headman's home and according to the forms described above, except for one involving drunkenness; in this instance the headman and five council members met at the foot of a coconut palm in the center of the village to hear charges by the owner of the tree that a neighbor was stealing the palm sap being collected in bamboo containers at the top of the tree. The accused was in the top of the tree, very drunk, during the course of the hearing, and gave his version of events while leaning out of the palm and drinking from the container of fermenting sap and shouting to be heard over the wind and the laughter of the onlookers. When he refused to come down at the end of the hearing, after a judgment of "drunk and disorderly," rather than a conviction for theft, the headman sent two boys up the palm to tie a line about the offender to secure him to the tree. He was fined one-eighth part of a *kerabau* and one small bowl, and left sleeping in the tree.

War

Settlement of disputes through use of armed force generally takes the form of a raid by a small group of men for the purpose of correcting an offense that cannot be dealt with in the structure of traditional law and justice. Such raids are called "headtaking of an enemy." Dusun warfare is generally caused by an individual from one descent group who is greatly offended at a major wrong supposedly done him by a person from another descent group. Major causes of such offense seem to be attacks with a knife, adultery, fraud, and theft. Raids also take place because of trespass or hunting and gathering by persons from one descent group on lands claimed by another descent group.

Raiding parties vary from 3 to 25 or more men, armed with wooden shields, blowpipes, and special fighting swords. Most raids are conducted at night. Victims are stabbed through the house floor or killed as the raiders dash into house sleeping areas. Quickly severing heads, and, if they have time, hands, the raiders retreat taking women or children captives if they can and whatever property that can be carried in full flight. The attacked community, feeling offended and embarrassed at the deaths, kidnapping, and loss of property, quickly organizes a large war party, prepares it with proper ritual, and sends it off to avenge the losses of the fight. A counterraid, also conducted at night, is expected and so the fighting is sharp. Losses of heads, hands, captives, and property in the counterraid are often as severe as in the initial battle.

After the first raid and counterraid full-scale fighting between large war parties becomes difficult because of the preparations on both sides for defense. Attacks tend then to be made by war parties on older women gathering food alone in the jungle, a solitary hunter, or children playing at the edge of a village.

On return to their village the raiding party usually hangs head and hand trophies, wrapped in leaf and rattan covers, on the lower branches of a special tree near the village area. Here they are greeted by female ritual specialists playing songs of victory upon a bamboo war flute, and by gong and drum music. Head and hand trophies are allowed to remain on the tree at least long enough for the flesh to rot away and then are put into a special trophy house until the triannual ritual of *mENebi,* celebrating past wrongs being righted through victory in war. Some head and hand trophies are placed in bamboo containers and hung in house eaves. The trophy structure, most often a small square platform raised on wooden posts, and roofed and sided with bamboo, is at a central location in the community. There it serves the purpose of a *tINAleg,* or symbol of "sacredness," and as a reminder of the bravery of village warriors in avenging offenses against traditional law. Age and sex determination of some 35 skull trophies present in 1959–1960 in the Sensuron trophy house gave an indication that much recent head-hunting warfare was directed against the aged, adolescents, and females; at least half the skulls were female, the majority being either young or very old, while some 10 percent of the remainder were adolescent boys.

The texts of ritual used in war ceremonies, songs, and folktales contain evidence that ritual cannibalism, involving the eating of special parts of a victim, was practiced on occasion in the recent past. Although head-hunting wars continue over several generations, a formal procedure can be employed to make peace when normal work and community life becomes impossible because of fear of raids. Descent group leaders representing warring villages meet on neutral ground to take an oath in the presence of a "peacemaker." The peacemaker is usually a leader of a descent group that has been neutral in the war. A series of ritual acts, including killing of several pigs to "cool offense in the universe," is performed at a site marked by a large special stone. That location is considered sacred if the oaths maintain peace between the warring groups, and may be used by other groups seeking to settle wars.

8

Subsistence and Economy

THE NATURAL WORLD about Sensuron is exploited by its people in three principal forms: (1) agriculture, (2) hunting and gathering of foods, and (3) gathering of raw materials for manufacture of clothing, shelter, and tools. A living in Sensuron is secured with reference to a detailed system of beliefs concerning proper techniques for obtaining, preparing, and using foodstuffs, shelter, clothing, and tools. Part of the task of getting a living is directed to exchange of some items obtained in subsistence activities for those produced by others.

Rice Agriculture

The primary crop grown by Dusun is rice, cultivated in one of two forms: (1) *swidden rice* ("slash and burn," "unirrigated," or "dry" rice) and, (2) *padi* ("wet" or "irrigated") *rice.* Rice agriculture in Sensuron is generally padi cultivation, with about 15 percent of the total rice crop grown in swidden fields on mountainsides about the village. Many Sensuron practices and beliefs about padi cultivation are derived from swidden cultivation.

The area of land exploited by a community in its agriculture, hunting, and gathering of foods, and extraction of raw material is bounded by a known set of physical markers. The boundary marks the property of the village, which is sometimes referred to by use of the term *pEmEgEnA,* a designation also commonly given to the particular section of land being swidden-farmed over a five-year period by a nuclear family household.

Swidden Agriculture Cycle

Swidden crops are planted in cleared mountainside plots of 3 to 15 acres. Each plot, or *sANkomAn,* is within the boundaries of one of the several *pEmEgEnA* of a nuclear family household. A *sANkomAn* is cleared and farmed each year for five years, until all plots available in a *pEmEgEnA* are used. Then land of a second *pEmEgEnA* is cleared, plot by plot, for each of five more years, until a move is made to a third *pEmEgEnA,* and, finally, in five more years to a fourth *pEmEgEnA.* At the end of the last five-year sequence of swidden cultivation, the practice is to return to farm the first *pEmEgEnA,* and begin the four-part, twenty-year-shifting cultivation cycle again. The twenty-year sequence is termed *gENguleAn,* "to return to the place where you first started."

Swidden agriculture is organized about a series of 11 major work activities, which begin in the period from late February to early March with *dEnmENAmut,* or "harvest." During this time 6 different types of work are recognized as important: (1) "to cut rice," (2) "to carry rice to a temporary field storehouse," (3) "to thresh grain from stalks through dancing," (4) "to thresh a second time to save rice grains," (5) "to winnow the small chaff from rice grains," and (6) "to carry the grain to the storehouse." Major ritual activities conducted by a female specialist take place when the rice is cut the first time and when it is carried to the permanent storehouse.

In the time from late March to early April of each year a ritual celebration of one to two weeks' duration is held to offer thanks to the rice spirit for success of the harvest and to insure a good crop in the next year. This ritual is conducted for individual households and the village by female ritual specialists.

The third part of the swidden cycle, "after harvest," begins with the planting of tobacco in early April and lasts through mid-May. Land is cleared separately from plots used in swidden cultivation. The crop is tended after planting by 12-to-15-year-old children who sit most of the day in a small, elevated, roofed bamboo structure located in the center of the plot, pulling upon long strands of rattan attached to bamboo rattles that are fixed upright in various parts of the field. The same scarecrow technique is used when the rice crop is maturing. The tobacco crop is usually harvested in July, processed by the men in the fall when the women are weeding rice fields, then taken to market the next year after harvest time. This part of the swidden cycle is occupied also by housebuilding, hunting, fishing, and village ceremonial activities concerned with head wars. It is also a period of leisure visiting within and between related villages.

In the weeks of May through June the fourth part of the swidden cycle, "to clear a field for rice planting," begins with the felling of trees and clearing of brush and plants. In this period close observation is made about 5 A.M. each morning to note the date of the first appearance of the Pleiades stars above the eastern horizon. This observation determines the time for burning the felled trees and brush in the swidden field. When the morning observation of Pleiades shows it to be at a point about 10 degrees above the horizon burning begins.

Then through the weeks of July the fifth part of the swidden cycle of agriculture occurs with burning of felled trees and bush. The firing process is dangerous in high winds and under very dry conditions, and is directed by an experienced male. When the first burning is completed, smaller, unburned tree trunks are pulled into piles and burned. Large trunks are left as they have fallen and the crop planted about them.

When the morning observation shows Pleiades has reached about a 70 degree elevation above the horizon, around September 1, the sixth part of the swidden cultivation cycle begins with "dibbling time," or planting of seeds in the plots. A short, pointed hardwood stick is used by the men to make a hole in the earth, into which five seeds are placed by the women. On completion of the planting a ritual is performed by the female specialist that insures growth of a healthy crop, and then a compost, or cover, of cut grass is laid over the newly planted field, and left there until the rice shoots are about one inch high.

In mid-September compost grasses are burned off the field to begin the seventh period of the cycle ("to burn compost"). At the end of September when the rice shoots are some six inches high, the eighth period of swidden activities, known as "the weeding," begins and lasts approximately a month. In the middle of October two cover crops are planted among the rows of rice plants. These provide shade for the young rice shoots. This time is a special occasion for feasting in the households and marks the midway point in the swidden cycle.

The period from early November to middle February, "the ear of rice is shooting," is the ninth stage of the swidden agricultural cycle. It is believed the rice is "pregnant" in this period. Weeding of the crop continues as a daily work activity of women. The tenth period, "to make scarecrows," or sometimes termed "sparrow chasing time," begins in mid-February. Weeding activity stops with the beginning of this period, and attention is given to protection of the swidden crop from birds and animals.

The eleventh period of the swidden cycle, which begins in late February to early March, depending on the maturity of the crop is "the time of the harvest offering." This period is primarily concerned with a ritual (*tumInpun*) by the female specialist, addressed to the rice spirit, in which a plea is made to the creator beings for aid in protecting the crop from harm by disease givers. A special form of *tINAleg,* called *sarApAk,* is carved from bamboo and planted in the middle of the swidden field with offerings to disease givers of eggs, rice, chicken, and salt. The tip of the *sarApAk* stick is opened out to hold the offerings and carved into a spear point to impale and kill disease givers as they attempt to take the ritual offerings. The installation of the *sarApAk* is followed by a household feast and several days to a week of rest while the crop matures fully. Then the harvest begins, ending the annual swidden agriculture cycle.

Each stage of the swidden cycle has one or more detailed ritual acts associated with it to insure the growth, yield, and protection of the crop. All rituals are conducted by female specialists.

Wet-Rice Agriculture

The eleven-part wet-rice agricultural cycle now practiced in Sensuron generally follows that used in swidden agriculture, varying in major detail where special techniques, such as preparing seed beds, transplanting, and irrigation practices, are used in growing this type of rice. The harvesting of wet rice begins in Sensuron in early January and lasts to mid-March of each year. The first two parts of the wet-rice agricultural cycle are identical with that of the swidden agricultural cycle. The third part of the wet-rice cycle—late March to early April—is also occupied with the same work and social tasks found in the swidden cycle: tobacco planting, house-building, hunting, fishing, ceremonial, and leisure-time activities. It is in the fourth part of the wet-rice cultivation cycle, "the winnowing time," that the first major difference between the two agricultural cycles appears. In the period from early April to the middle of April the newly harvested grain is laid out on drying mats and sifted to eliminate chaff and debris of harvest. Such work is done usually by women, while men either hunt and fish or work at house repair and building.

The fifth division occurs from the middle to the end of April with repair or rebuilding by men of the rice storehouses. The sixth part of the cycle, "to plant seedlings," occupies the time from early May to mid-July. Three major work activities occur in sequence in this part of the wet-rice cycle: (1) "to cut grass for a nursery," (2) " to make a fence about seedlings," and (3) "to plant seedlings." Women do the weeding for the nursery using a wooden-handled, metal-bladed hoe, while men do cutting of bamboo and rattan materials and building of fences. Both sexes participate in the labor of planting seedlings, with men doing dibbling and women planting seeds. Seed nurseries in Sensuron are either cut out of small land areas unused for cultivation, such as the edges of the village burial ground or put in the middle of the wet-rice land. The amount of seed planted depends upon the size of the fields to be sown. A one-acre wet-rice field is said to require 3.5 gallons of seed in a nursery of 18 by 30 feet, while a two-acre field is supposed to require 7 gallons of seed in a nursery measuring 65 by 30 feet. Most seed nurseries have scarecrows placed about them, with older children and young adults assigned to take care of the seedlings.

The seventh period of this cycle begins in mid-July and lasts through late August. This time or "the preparation of the padi irrigation dikes," involves three work activities. The work sequence is: (1) "to cut grass at the corners of fields and along irrigation channels," (2) "to cut grass along padi dikes, and (3) "to repair padi dikes." The wet-rice fields used in Sensuron are generally located at the foot of the river bluff alongside the community and have been cleared from primary jungle. The fields vary in size from one to five acres, are bounded and cross-cut by earthen dikes shaped along the contours of the land. Dikes are built up about 30 inches and are 18 to 24 inches thick at the base. The fields are irrigated through a complex system of earth channels and wood and bamboo conduits.

The main earth channels are 4 to 5 feet deep and 3 feet across, and dug in a manner that allows water to move swiftly through them. There are several areas of fields where the padi dikes create terraces across the face of hillsides, with irrigation water flowing down through the dikes and spilling over their tops. The longest irrigation system in use in Sensuron involves a main channel of just under two miles and three sections where water is transported across ravines by flumes made of hollowed tree trunks and bamboo. There is a complex system of measuring irrigation water to be shared and a set of beliefs concerning rights to shared irrigation waters. Weeding, repair, and maintainence of padi dikes in the seventh period of the cycle is the task of women, using hoes to reshape and rebuild the dikes with earth taken from the foot of the wall, then patting it down with the sole of a foot. During this time men prepare plows and harnesses for use in the next period of work.

The eighth part of the wet-rice cultivation, beginning in late August and lasting through mid-September, "plowing," involves three major work activities: (1) first plowing, (2) second plowing, (3) carrying away grass. For three to seven days at the beginning of this period water is allowed to flood the fields, to soften the ground for plowing. When the ground has softened, *kerabou* are brought into the fields and used to pull a thick wood plow (3 by 4 feet by 6 inches), with 3-inch-long wooden teeth set in rows along the underside. The plow, or *rAgus,* is attached to the animal with rattan lines leading to a carved wooden neck yoke, and is used by a male standing on top of the plow, while driving the *kerabou* about the field. A second and third animal, plowing separately, are usually employed in the first period of field preparation. When the ground has been turned over to the point where the surface is ankle to knee deep mud, the second plowing is done, often with teams of *kerabou* being walked over the field. The animals are tied with their noses to the flank of a *kerabou* ahead, with the group of three to six *kerabou* driven in a counterclockwise fashion about the field. When the second plowing is completed fields are flooded for several days, and then the grass and debris from plowing are gathered from the water surface and irrigation system and piled to dry. The time of plowing is one of labor for all adults in a household, with younger children participating by riding as passengers on the plow to give weight in turning up the earth.

The ninth period, "the planting time," begins in mid-September and continues until early October and consists of three major work activities: (1) "to dam fields for irrigation," (2) "to carry seedlings," (3) "to transplant seedlings." Transplanting work is divided between men and women; generally women take up the seedlings and carry them in special baskets from the nursery to the field area, and men help plant, working alongside women. Planting is done through use of a dibble stick. Rice shoots are held in one hand while the dibble stick is driven into the mud; then the seedlings are planted with special care given to proper spacing between each planting.

The tenth period, known as "the weeding time," lasts from completion of planting through November. The eleventh period, "the time to prepare for harvest," begins about the first of December and lasts until harvesting begins in early January. During this time three work activities occupy the adults of Sensuron: (1) "to make rice mats," (2) "to gather sago palm leaves for weaving into a roof of a temporary rice store, and (3) "to cut bamboo and make a temporary field store." The weaving of mats is a woman's task, while men gather sago palm fronds, cut bamboo, and construct a field rice storehouse. The ritual of *tumInpun* marks the close of the period and is in the same form used in the swidden cycle.

As in the swidden cultivation cycle, each stage of the wet-rice cycle has one or several ritual acts associated with it. Each of the 15 rituals regularly used are concerned with protection or growth and yield of the rice crop. All are conducted by female ritual specialists.

Harvest is a time of holiday for the people of Sensuron. Work preparations for harvesting and the labor of the harvest are taken on at increased tempo and with general good humor. The tensions building up between neighbors tend to decrease, and the atmosphere of most social activities is less tense, with a reduced amount of concern over poisoning, magical efforts to change luck, and suspension of old arguments.

Economics of Rice Agriculture

It is believed in Sensuron that each adult must be provided with at least three *tAmpurAN,* or half coconut shells, per day of uncooked rice (*pari*) for maintaining normal activities. Each child is supposed to need two cups of *pari* each day. The normal measure of a *gAntEN,* or gallon by dry measure, is calculated to be 14 *tAnpurAN,* or cups of *pari.* Thus, each adult is supposed to need 6 gallons of *pari* each month for food, while each child should be provided with 4 gallons per month of *pari.* With a yearly minimum need of 72 to 80 gallons of *pari* for each adult and 48 to 50 gallons of *pari* for each child, a household of three adults and two children would have to secure at least 300 gallons of rice to maintain what is believed a normal diet. Also, an average family of five persons is supposed to have at least 195 gallons additional supplies of *pari* to feed animals, to provide for seed for the next crop, and to use for ritual and social purposes.

The average nuclear family household in Sensuron is said to have to secure a minimum of 500 gallons of *pari* each harvest. In 1960 a study of the wet-rice agriculture yield was conducted in Sensuron as reported for the 183 village households. Specific measures were taken in 26 households as a check of validity of reporting after the first cutting and again after the first winnowing of the grain. There is a 10 percent loss of grain in the winnowing process. There is a further 10 to 15 percent reduction of the grain amount in the act of husking. Data for the yield of *pari* per household show that approximately 10 percent of the 183 village households appear not to have secured enough rice to meet the basic subsistence need of 72 gallons per adult and 48 gallons per child in the household, and had no surpluses for feeding animals, ritual, or social purposes. The remaining households gained a yield of *pari* from the 1960 harvest distributed as follows: 40 percent of the village households secured one times more than the basic food need of *pari;* 28 percent of the households secured two times more than the basic need; 8 percent of the households secured three times more than the basic need; while the remaining 14 percent of the households secured between four and five times more than the basic food needs. However, when the basic subsistence need is adjusted to include the nearly 200 gallon extra amount of *pari* felt required for animals, ritual, and social purposes, approximately one quarter of Sensuron households did not secure an amount of *pari* considered adequate by village definition.

A study of the actual time spent in labor for rice agriculture by six households in Sensuron provides a figure of an average of 57 days of labor for each person of the six households working on each acre of wet rice, with four to ten days more than the average occurring in those instances where the fields were distant, soils rocky, slopes steep, adequate water lacking for irrigation, and some clearing of brush had to be undertaken.

These figures clearly indicate differences in income from agricultural activities and provide indications of the way social status based in wealth in rice occurs in Sensuron. Over a period of years, providing no diseases affect the crop or the health of household members, a surplus of rice can be accumulated that lends substance to opinion of high economic status in the village. At least ten families in Sensuron had stocks of rice stored that could allow them to miss between six and ten harvests without reducing their high levels of consumption of *pari*. On the other hand, as many households in the village regularly were without rice for food in the two months before harvest. For most households in Sensuron the facts of economic life and social status are quite simple: the rich in rice seem to get richer and more affluent, while the poor remain poor.

Gardening

Most nuclear family households in Sensuron prepare and plant gardens for raising foods and cultivate a variety of trees and shrubs for their fruits, nuts, berries, and other edible products. Also, they often cultivate flowering and ornamental plants, shrubs, and trees for medical uses and as decoration of the household location. Specialized cultivation occurs of plants whose fibers are used in making cloth, baskets, and tools. Nearly all gardening activities are conducted by women. The major exception is the recent cultivation by men of rubber trees as a cash crop. All plants cultivated, for whatever purposes, are individually owned by the persons or households planting them.

Gardening activities are devoted to raising more than 25 food stuffs, including plantings of the sweet potato, greater yam, manioc (tapioca), bottle-gourd, mung bean, garlic, elephant's ear, tomato, melon, squash, chili pepper, onion, ginger, betel pepper, cow pea, corn, mustard, peanut, pineapple, watermelon, eggplant, sugar cane, and cabbage. The sweet potato, yam, and manioc are planted in quantity as major supplements to rice in daily eating.

At the borders of garden areas and adjacent to houses the people of Sensuron cultivate trees and shrubs bearing coconuts, bananas, breadfruit, mango, papaya, malay apple, durian, limes, citrus fruits, and coffee beans. The sago palm is planted for both food and materials used in manufactures. Some half dozen plants are cultivated near houses or adjacent to garden plots for use in manufacture of tools, shelter, and clothing. These plants include bamboo, cotton, kapok (or silk cotton tree), betel palm, common gourds, indigo, and derris.

The bamboo, cotton, kapok, and betel palm are the more important plants cultivated, and of these bamboo is used most commonly. It can be said that in 1959–1960 Sensuron was a community living in a bamboo world. Most house materials were of bamboo, as were many tools, including a variety of weapons, most containers, and many musical instruments. Too, bamboo shoots were regularly eaten as foods.

Hunting and Gathering

The hunting and gathering of foods in the primary jungle, as well as extracting raw materials for manufacture of shelter, tools, clothing, and medicines, are also important subsistence activities in Sensuron.

Most animals of the jungle are considered edible and are killed by hunters. The only exceptions are those believed to be omen givers, such as the woodpeckers, or those animals, such as the cobra and wildcat, considered too dangerous to kill at close quarters with the weapons the Dusun use. Primary concern in hunting is given to larger meat animals, such as the pig, deer, ant eater, bear, gibbon, orangutan, and monkey. A major class of rituals, *pEsusubAk id puru* ("sacred water for luck in the jungle"), which includes four ritual forms, is used by hunters to insure their luck and safety in the hunt. Most hunting is done with packs of eight to ten specially trained dogs. The blowpipe and poison darts, spear, knife, and club are major hunting weapons. A wide use is made of some ten types of bamboo and rattan spear and noose traps, especially in capturing game such as rats, pigs, and monkeys.

Fishing and gathering of marine animals also occupy time in subsistence activities. Bamboo traps in varying sizes are placed in most streams about the village, in irrigation channels, and even in the wet-rice fields at points where water flows through dikes. A substantial amount of fishing with woven fiber nets, lines, and poles is also conducted by men and women. A wide range of materials are gathered from the jungle for use as food and for manufacture of tools, clothing, and shelter. These materials include rattan, bamboo, hardwoods, tree barks, fruits, vegetables, and a great variety of insects, worms, and small animals.

Domestic Animals

A variety of domestic animals are used in Sensuron as sources of food, power, and material. Several have important value in ritual activities. The chicken and duck are common fowl, with some geese tended in a few households. Pigs and *kerabou* are kept by all households. Dogs and cats are found in most houses as pets. The chicken, pig, and *kerabou* are important in ritual uses, as well as basic sources of meat. As noted, the *kerabou* is also a key animal in wet-rice agriculture. Dogs are used as hunting tools, and cats are kept to hunt jungle rats infesting the household and rice storehouses.

Material Culture

It has been noted that bamboo provides much of the raw material for tools, containers, weapons, clothing, and shelter in Sensuron. Selected jungle hardwoods and rattan are the other major items of raw material used in manufacture of material culture items. A little work is done in bone and some stone tools are worked. Clay is used primarily to shape cooking pots.

Bamboo, split out and dried flat, provides 10-to-15-inch-wide sections varying from 4 to 50 feet in length for use in house building. Split in half and cut into 4-foot lengths bamboo becomes roof tiles. Cut at the joint with the next section, bamboo provides a watertight container holding from a half pint to a half gallon of water or a pound of pickled meat and rice. Split into sections, it is carved into knife blades, mouth harps, hair pins, clothing clasps, and eating utensils. Shredded into strips, bamboo is used for weaving hats, mats, and more than 15 types of trays and containers for holding and transporting nearly everything used in daily life; sharpened and hardened in a fire, it becomes a spear tip with razor-sharp edges. Built into several sections, it becomes a piston bellows for use in metal forging.

Bamboo is used principally to weave the frame of a complex rice-husking mill. It serves as food, as needle for sewing, a shuttle for weaving, a comb for cording cotton and kapok, a blowpipe poison dart case, a ritual device to show a sacred location, an ownership symbol, as a drill in making blowpipes and other weapons and tools, a coffin, fencing, and barriers to disease givers.

Hardwoods and their barks are used to make houseposts; cross supports for floors, blowpipes, spear, axe and knife handles, plows and yokes, children's toy tops, house steps, as a pestle and mortar used in husking rice, cloth for men's jackets, and the sides of rice store bins.

The rattan gathered in the jungle serves as the tie device in most Sensuron manufacture. More than 20 knots, some simple and many very complex, are used to tie bamboo to hardwood house frames, to lash handles to weapons and containers, and to tie bundles, baskets, and animals; rattan rope is used for lines in *kerabau* plowing, tethering, and slaughter. Hunters bind their kills onto carrying baskets or poles with rattan; nearly everything held together is bound with rattan of some form.

Marketing

The products of subsistence activity are regularly exchanged at markets held at meeting points between Sensuron and nearby friendly villages. Informal marketing of products occurs within the village, usually between neighborhoods. And two or three times each year parties are organized to carry products through the jungle mountains to trading centers at the seacoast. Traders traveling through the village on regular trips also bargain for scarce subsistence products.

Marketing surplus or scarce subsistence products is conducted within the framework of general beliefs concerning property and its exchange or transmission (see Chapter 7). At weekly or semimonthly markets goods are placed on bamboo mats for display. Rice is rarely exchanged in any form. Products marketed are either manufactured items or foods in season, particularly vegetables and fruits, or scarce products collected in the jungle or streams. Thus a row of 15 or 20 mats set down in the shade of coconut palms at the edge of a stream will generally display the same fruits or vegetables. Individual mats will have a few rare jungle fruits, nuts, or berries; salt; or specially desired pieces of hardwood or lengths of rattan. Occasionally a hunter's wife will display dried or pickled meats. For the most part women conduct all marketing activities centering about display mats. Groups of men cluster near persons displaying manufactured items for sale or offering major items of inheritable property, particularly gongs and earthenware jars. Manufactured items displayed by men tend to be those made only by men; blowpipes, darts, dart cases, spears, knife and axe handles, plows and yokes, and a variety of musical instruments. Items made primarily by women, such as baskets, trays, and clothing, are marketed only by women.

Salt has been used as a medium of exchange for small items, when a direct exchange of goods was not possible or desired. Marketing days usually end with quick exchanges of equivalent items, without much discussion of price, since the values of fruits or vegetables generally are the same.

Markets are well attended, even in seasons of heaviest subsistence work, and are times for exchange of news, gossip, and, on occasion, a hearing by the village leaders of a descent group to settle a dispute between villages or persons from different villages concerning a violation of traditional law. A substantial amount of rice wine and coconut toddy is passed about, and the early morning market often stretches on into a relaxed late afternoon of small talk, joking, and making of plans for cooperative work.

9

Life Experience and World View

THIS FINAL CHAPTER is a brief account of the routine of life in Sensuron. In it an attempt is also made to portray the meanings of certain life experiences for the people of the village and it ends with a brief discussion of culture change.

In the paragraphs that follow, as in the preceding chapters, a description is given of the way life in Sensuron impresses an observer from a Western European society. It should be recognized that the words used in this text to characterize the community and the customary behavior of its people are from a Western language that is rooted in a life and cultural historical experience very different from those of the Dusun of Sensuron. The people of the village do not view their lives or beliefs in Western terms. No modern ethnographer would make the error of confusing his impressions, and descriptions based on impressions, with those of the people he studies. To do so would be to make the fundamental error of most studies of customary behavior of the past century and that is still made at present by many travelers, government officials, and missionaries. To attribute meanings from the observer's life to the forms of behavior witnessed in a native community is to destroy whatever objectivity there is to be gained by a human being serving as an instrument of observation. I am aware that all the people of Sensuron do not all think and act in all the ways I will have described. I believe one of my tasks as an ethnographer is to try to learn as best I can the major categories of belief and customary behavior widely held in a society and then to describe them as clearly and simply as possible. The problem of this last chapter, as it has been generally through the book, is to provide some feeling of Dusun life to members of my own society without rendering the account meaningless to those members of Dusun society who may read it.

Routines of Living

Sensuron is astir an hour before the dawn of most mornings. It is usually too damp and cold to sleep. Fires are built up and the morning meal cooked while members of the household cluster about the house fire-pit seeking warmth.

After eating, containers and utensils are rinsed off with water to "keep the worms off" and replaced in racks on the side of the house porch. Older children are sent to the river to carry water home in bamboo containers, while their mother spends her time gathering together equipment for the day's work, including some cold rice wrapped in leaves for a midday snack. The men and adolescent males go into the yard to sit in the first warmth of the sun and talk with male neighbors. The early morning exchange of plans, news, and recounting of the events of yesterday is considered a "proper way" to begin the day. While the men cluster in the yard center, with old shirts or cloths draped about bare shoulders to ward off the chill, women gather in front of one house or another, also trading news, gossip, and work plans. Many women comb each other's hair, after carefully picking out the lice. It is not unusual to see four or more women sitting in a row down the steps of a house ladder talking, while combing and delousing hair. Babies are nursed while mothers talk and small children run about the clusters of adults, generally being ignored until screams of pain or anger cause a sharp retort of *kAdA!* (do not!) from a parent. Women drape spare skirts about their bare shoulders to ward off the morning chill. About two hours after dawn these groups break up as the members go off to the work of the day. The work tasks of each day are those to be done under the annual cycle of subsistence labor, described in the previous chapter.

If it is a rest day or a time when bad omens make it unwise to be about work tasks, men continue to sit in the sun, talking and working often at small tasks, such as sharpening knives, carving knife handles or sheaths, or repairing some item of work equipment. Men also engage in cooperative personal grooming during these leisure times, shaping and trimming hair, occasionally making a tattoo, and sometimes shaving unwanted facial hair from the face of a relative or friend. By the middle of the day men have retired to the houses where they lounge and sleep until late afternoon.

Women may spend another hour in the yard in the early morning if they do not go off to work in fields and gardens or go jungle gathering. By midmorning, however, they have gone into the houses, where they busy themselves with the tasks of cooking and preparation of food, particularly the husking of rice with a long wooden pestle pounded into a wood block with a bowl-shaped depression in the center that is filled with rice; if the family owns a rice mill, the husking is done with this tool. Women usually prepare rice only for the meals of one day, for it is considered unlucky and offensive to the rice spirit to have surpluses of husked rice that are not to be eaten in a day. At harvest and other times when work must begin at dawn, women begin pounding rice at 3 and 4 A.M.; the rhythmic husking beat, echoing with a thump onto and through the bamboo house floor, is a sound of life in Sensuron. During the afternoons of leisure days, while the men rest, women generally work at weaving rice mats or winnowing trays and baskets.

Leisure time conversations are carried on with some intensity, but with humor. Dusun enjoy taking descriptions of familiar events and objects and placing them together in conversation to form ridiculous combinations, and are quick to turn a serious comment to a pun or joke with a fast quip. Sexual joking is common and becomes highly ribald at times. A favorite leisure-time activity for men is pitting specially trained roosters against one another, while making wagers on the outcome of the fight. A crowd of a 100 or more men and boys will surround a rooster fight on many leisure days, shouting encouragement to their favorite, and helping inspect and soothe a defeated animal. Property is wagered on the fights, sometimes in substantial amounts.

There are decorative and representational art forms in use in the village, in naturalistic carvings of wooden utensils and house doors, and in symbolic designs woven into cloth, hats, and baskets. This work is done by individuals for their own use. Hat and cloth designs are distinctive of villages and areas, and are special sources of pride to women who make them. Designs are most often done in a curvilinear or spiral motif, typical of other Borneo peoples. Some carving of ritual objects becomes elaborate in decoration. Generally the people of Sensuron give much more attention to music, dancing, and verse forms. As noted, instrumental music by gongs and drums is an important part of village ritual and social life. A variety of stringed and wind instruments of bamboo and rattan construction also are used in music. Most men play most of the instruments and are proficient in the use of one. Many women are skilled in use of stringed and wind instruments, but do not play either gongs or drums. Female ritual specialists are proficient usually in use of bamboo flutes.

Vocal music is a common feature of village life; mothers and grandmothers sing a great variety of lullabies and "growth songs" to babies, children sing a wide range of traditional and nonsense songs, while adults sing at work in the fields and gardens, during leisure and social occasions and at times of ritual. Drinking songs and wedding songs take elaborate forms, often in the nature of song "debates" with sides chosen and a winner declared by a host or guest of honor on the basis of "beauty" of tone, humor, and general "one-upmanship" in invention of new verse forms. Most group singing is done in harmony. Adolescents, especially girls, spend much of their solitary leisure time singing traditional songs of love and loneliness. Traditional verse forms in ritual, and extensive everyday use of riddles, folktales, and proverbs comprise a substantial body of oral literature. Many persons know much ritual verse, and most can recite dozens of stylized folktales, riddles, and proverbs.

Village headmen, certain older males, and ritual specialists of both sexes are practiced speechmakers. A skill of "speaking beautifully" is much admired and imitated. The style used involves narration, with exhortation, and is emphasized through voice tone and many hand and body gestures and postures. Political debates, court hearings, and personal arguments often become episodes of dramatic representation for onlookers, with a speaker's every phrase listened to for its emotional expressive content and undertones of ridicule, tragedy, comedy, and farce at the expense of others involved. The verse forms of major rituals take on dimensions of drama as the specialist delivers the lines with skillful impersonations of voices and mannerisms of disease givers, souls of the dead, and creator beings.

By late afternoon of a leisure day people in the houses begin to drift to the yards, where they again sit and talk. Fires are built to ward off the chill of winds rising off the mountains, and men and women circle the blaze, throwing bits of wood and bamboo into the fire as they talk. This time is termed *mEg-Amut,* after the designation for exchange of small talk between household members. As many as 20 fires can be seen burning in yards through Sensuron at evening on most leisure days and on many evenings after work periods. Men sit and talk until after dark, when they go into houses to take their evening meal. Women leave about an hour before dark to prepare the meal. Smaller children usually eat before the adults. After the evening meal, for an hour or more, the family clusters about the house fire-pit, talking, with adults often engaged in small tasks of tool repair or manufacture. By 8 or 9 P.M. most families are asleep; the time of retiring is earlier when the work days are long, later on rest days.

Little drinking of rice wine takes place during most leisure-time activities, and very little household visiting occurs. The yard area is a common meeting place and the main point of neighborhood contact. Few persons go into other households to drink, relax, or chat. The nature of the outdoors exchange of news and gossip is such that gossips are called *rAgAN tAnA* or "red earth buttocks" since they go from area to area in the village hearing and spreading tales while sitting in the red clay of the yards.

The routine of a work day varies through the year, as adults go to gardens or fields, or to the jungle for hunting and gathering. It is rare for a single adult, other than a hunter and those away on long trips, to be gone from the village overnight while working. Most adults are at home by midafternoon, after a bath in the river. On rest days baths usually are taken an hour or so later. Men and women bathe separately, with men removing all clothing and women bathing in a sarong. Usually, 7-to-12-year-old children take baths at various times of the day, as play groups swim in the river. Adolescents bathe at the end of the day as do adults. Young children accompany their mother in her bath. Most often the youngest children are taken by a mother to her work in the field or garden, where they play on and about a rice mat set in the shade of a nearby tree. Older children are left at home, to play in and about the house, under care of an adolescent or an aged relative. When there are no persons to watch children, it is not uncommon for a mother to lock her young children in the household while she spends the day at work.

Members of a household sleep in the area about the fire-pit, often with the parents nearest the fire and children at varying distances from them.The youngest child often sleeps between his parents. Some households have one or two sleeping rooms at one end of the house for use by visitors. Most often these are used for storage of rice or equipment. Most people sleep on a mat of woven bamboo, often laid over thick wooden planks to prevent being stabbed through the floor from beneath the house while asleep. Many persons use pillows of cotton cloth stuffed with kapok, some have cloth and kapok coverlets. Most people sleep in their clothing, draping spare clothes over themselves for warmth. It is often an hour before the family finally settles into sleep, since children and adults talk as they rest on their mats at the fire's edge.

A village house is usually one rectangular room, with a small attached structure for storage. The average size of the house is 15 by 25 feet. Houses are built up 3 to 4 feet from the ground on hardwood posts with frames of hardwood poles. Bamboo is split and tied with rattan to the framework to form walls and laid to make a floor. Half bamboo sections are laid to form a "Spanish tile" type roof. Inside the house there are some small hardwood seating blocks, and gongs, jars, and weapons that are placed against or hung alongside walls. A raised seating platform often runs the length of one wall of the house. Rolled bedding is stuffed into a corner, often next to a large wooden chest, which is usually secured with a wood toggle and rattan. The chest contains valued items of clothing, beads, rings, and so on. A few houses have a platform built under the roof on which gongs, jars, and wood chests are stored, and which may be used by adolescents for sleeping. There is only one door always opening onto a large, roofed porch. Windows are at a minimum in most houses, for fear of disease givers and souls of the dead. Many houses have windows cut with bamboo bars left in the opening, in the belief that harmful spirts cannot enter through such barriers. Doors and windows are kept tightly shut and covered most of the time, so houses are usually dark in the interior. However, enough light filters through bamboo walls to allow movement and to carry on most work tasks. When the family is absent the door is tied with a toggle that can be released by reaching through the door frame.

There are no special provisions for personal hygiene in village houses. water for drinking and rinsing of food utensils and washing hands and faces is kept in bamboo containers hung on the porch. Adults usually urinate at the side or rear of the house. Adults walk away from houses to nearby locations used for defecation. Pigs and dogs often follow to clean up body wastes. Children are "toilet trained" by mothers holding them over the porch edge. Until about five years of age children eliminate at this location. After this age they are urged by parents to follow the habits of the adults and move to the side of the house or to the bushes nearby.

It is believed a meal must not be eaten without rinsing hands and mouth of "worms" and other diseases. At meal times a family will first crowd the porch, squatting down, while pouring water over each other's hands, drinking, gargling, and spitting vigorously.

The people of Sensuron use a variety of bodily positions in standing, while relaxing, and when recumbent. Both sexes stand with feet planted firmly and widely, arms loose at the side. Men relax while squatting down so that their buttocks rest against the calves of their legs, holding their hands loosely, with arms draped over the knees. Women sit on the ground in one of several positions, most commonly with legs crossed, arms draped across knees, and hands held loosely. The favored sleeping position is to curl on one side, with knees pulled up, and both hands tucked between the thighs.

Life Cycle

In Sensuron people usually deal with their sex drives through ideally denying their existence, while often behaving in ways designed to sidestep social and cultural barriers to personal satisfaction. At the ideal level of belief the view is expressed that "men are not like dogs, chasing any bitch in heat," or "sex relations are unclean." Some of the sexuality of Dusun life has been noted earlier. There is a high content of lewd and bawdy behavior in the play of children and adolescents, and in the behavior of adults. For example, the eight-year-old girl in the house across from ours was angrily ordered by her mother to come into the house to help in rice husking. The girl turned to her mother and gave her a slow, undulating thrust of her hips in a sexual sign. More than 12 salacious gestures are known and used regularly by children and adults of both sexes, and there are some 20 equivalents of "four-letter" English terms specifically denoting the sexual anatomy and its possible uses. Late one afternoon 4 girls between 8 and 15 years, and 2 young boys of 4 and 5 years were chasing about our house steps for a half hour, grabbing at each others genitals, and screaming "there is your mother's vulva!" Adult onlookers were greatly amused at the group and became convulsed with laughter when the four-year-old boy improvised the answer, "my mother has no vulva!" Thus, sexual behavior is supposed to be unclean and disgusting, while in reality it is a source of amusement and constant attention.

Unmarried women often use facial cosmetics of a variety of types to enhance their desirability, and dress in forms calculated to lure male attention. An unmarried woman should cover her breasts at all times. Once married, and a mother, she may dispense with a blouse about the house. Unmarried girls arrange blouses in such a manner as to emphasize their breasts. Unmarried boys and many adult males spend much leisure time joking and speculating concerning the shape and firmness of the breasts of a particular girl.

A variety of acts by women are interpreted as having erotic meaning, including uses of glances and particular inclinations of the head and body motions. When rice wine is served at parties, it is the usual practice to have unmarried girls distribute cups to men. Married women seeking a temporary sexual liaison will join in the distribution to signal their sexual availability, and often set off a public argument with their husbands. A touching of hands when cups are passed is considered an invitation to intercourse, and often leads to sexual acts in the dark near the house.

Children learn details of sexual behavior early, and sex play is a part of the behavior of four-to-six-year olds, usually in houses or rice storehouses while parents are away at work. Older children engage in sexual activities in groups and pairs, often at a location outside the village, in an abandoned field storehouse, or in a temporary shelter in a remote garden. Most girls are initiated to sexual intercourse before 12, usually by boys of 14 to 16 years of age, and sometimes by young men. Many girls have intercourse regularly with a number of boys before their marriage. Most boys have intercourse with a variety of girls before marriage. Usually boys of 12 to 14 are initiated to sexual activities by a girl of 15 to 17 who is the regular partner of a group of boys of that age.

Comment was made earlier concerning extramarital sexual relations. Several male informants noted that with the exceptions of their own wives most women in the village are known to have had several sexual liaisons outside of marriage. Village women are convinced that their husbands engage in adulterous relations regularly. The incidence of extramarital sexual behavior is difficult to judge accurately, but it appears to be a regular feature of village life.

It is believed a man or woman's duty is to marry and have children. A bachelor or spinster is considered to be "unfair," and it is commonly said of such persons, *AtEbAt au AsAkog,* "they have wasted themselves in not having children."

There is no isolation of or tabus for a menstruating female, although generally women "feel ashamed" if it should be known that they are menstruating. Yet women are proud of menses, for it is believed a sign of ability to conceive and bear children. Inability to bear children is a serious matter, always the fault of a woman, and a cause for divorce. Adults consider the numbers of their children to be a symbol of increasing age; it is not uncommon for a parent to say, *m-ElEhIN Egumul tanak!,* "I have great age for I have many children!" However, women dislike the menopause, for they know it signals the end of ability to bear children. Once this time has been reached, a woman will class herself as "very old" and "about to die," and seek ritual relief to begin her menses again, for generally it is believed a child is conceived from the intermixture of the "blood" of the male and female. The process of fetal growth is explained as the blood of the mother boiling about the belly, with drops of "steam" forming and collecting to shape the child's body. A bride will eat specially cooked foods to enhance both her ability to conceive and the ability of her blood to steam and form a child, *miEguiEm Em marEnarE,* "to grow upwards and outwards."

It is felt that ideally a child is equally the product of both parents, although the man is considered solely responsible for conception in cases of illegitimacy. However, wives are teased by husbands with the expression, "Don't be unkind to me; I am needed to start the children!", and mothers warn harsh fathers, "Do not beat that child you have made!"

A woman is supposed to be able to tell she is pregnant by her sudden aversion to favorite foods or by her special desires for "sour" foods. It is believed the boiling blood of pregnancy causes illness leading to some food aversions and food desires that warn a woman to take care to avoid certain acts and omens which bring bad luck in pregnancy and birth. When a woman does not "feel aversion," it is common for her husband to assume this activity on her behalf; he cannot eat the food prohibited to pregnant women, and must take care to avoid omens of ill-fortune. This act of "taking the woman's place" is felt necessary to protect the mother and child, and it is not considered at all unusual for men to refuse foods with the expression, "I cannot for the baby."

Turtles and owls are felt especially bad omens for a pregnant woman; a turtle symbolizes a miscarriage, an owl a difficult birth. A variety of foods cannot be eaten and most pregnant women suffer cravings for special food items, such as mango, lemons, or certain meats, which usually are obtained and prepared by their husbands. A pregnant woman is not expected to ride a *kerabou,* to avoid a miscarriage supposed to result from motion. Pregnant females are allowed to continue work in fields and gardens, for it is said to be "good" for the rice and other foods to be shown fertility. The sex of the child is predicted from fetal movement. If the movement is rough and rapid, it is a girl; if movements are gentle, the baby is to be a boy.

Sickness in pregnancy is treated by the female specialist with applications of medicinal plants felt to lead to "cooling of the blood." Women bearing their first children are warned specially "to be very careful to observe customs" by their mothers and mothers-in-law. In subsequent pregnancies a woman can dispense with some observances of this period, for she supposedly "knows her own strength" and will not become sick easily.

Childbirth in Sensuron is a private event, attended only by a midwife, who may be a female ritual specialist, the woman's mother, or her husband's mother. A location is selected near the "upper wall of the house," (the wall towards the upper side of the hill upon which the house is built) and an ordinary sleeping mat is spread out for the mother to kneel upon while she holds on to a strap of bark-cloth line suspended from a roof beam. The midwife kneels before the mother and massages her back and abdomen in the final stages of labor and takes the child at birth. The baby is given to the father's mother or to the wife's mother to be bathed in warm water and wrapped in a special cloth. With a specially made bamboo knife the cord is severed and with the afterbirth it is placed in a bamboo container that is sealed and hung under the porch eaves as a sign of a birth in the household. The cord is cut to special measures for boys and girls; the cord is stretched to a girl's nasal bridge and cut at that point, whereas for boys it is stretched over the forehead as far as it will reach and then cut. It is believed that girls are destined to be "short tempered" so the cord can be cut short. Boys are felt to be better off being "long tempered" so the cord is cut as long as possible to avoid them being *baroken* ("a bad tempered male").

It is believed that difficult births need a special ritual to protect the child and mother, and the ritual is conducted by the female specialist as the mother bears down in delivery. Unusual presentations of the child are felt caused by a mother's illness in pregnancy due to a bad omen or violation of food and work tabus and are treated only through ritual. Caul births are considered most fortunate events, for it is believed that as the child is protected by the caul membrane so he will be invincible to disease, accident, and in war.[1]

The personal effects of the wife and household equipment used in delivery are taken to the river and washed by the father. Contact with these materials is felt especially dangerous to unmarried girls and to other pregnant women due to danger of disease or malformations at birth. Husbands often hire a female neighbor to do the washing, paying a special ritual fine as well as a wage in rice.

Respiration is initiated through massaging the cord, hands, and chest of the baby. Once breathing is regular and the cord cut, the child is bathed and a special medicinal lotion is applied to the baby's umbilical area, which is bound with a cloth, with the intent of "curing the cord," or closing off a possible source for entry of the childbirth disease *AuenkAt*. This sickness is brought to either a new mother or newborn on the rays of the sun and winds, or through

[1] The inner fetal membrane of higher vertebrates sometimes is not ruptured at birth and so covers the head of the baby until cleared away.

acts of the disease givers attracted to the house by the smell of blood and birth. For a period of either eight or ten days the mother and child are isolated in the house from all contacts except those with the nuclear family and the wife's mother and father. The child must not be touched by other persons in this time, since they may harbor *AuenkAt* or be possessed temporarily by a disease giver seeking disguise to come near the mother and child. The eight-day isolation period, or *mENgErIntud,* is favored over the ten-day period, because "the unlucky number eight fools the disease givers into thinking the child is dead, and so they go away."

The infant is the sole concern of his mother during his first 30 days of life as she bathes, nurses, and coddles him with special lullabies and growth songs. During this month at least six ritual acts are performed by the female specialist for the infant to promote his well-being and growth. Between the fourth and second day after birth the ritual of *pEgedu sEmubu* is said to appease disease givers angry at their inability to get at the mother's milk because of her isolation. On the 4th through the 6th day after birth the ritual of *lAntAdAk* is said to enable the mother to move freely about the house at work tasks, while the infant sleeps on its mat. At the fourth day after a birth a specialist recites another ritual, while a mother clothes the infant in a specially woven cloth believed to provide magical protection. Between the eighth and fourteenth day after birth, depending on the date of actual termination of the period of isolation, a lengthy ritual is performed, to provide strength for the child and mother when they come in contact with disease givers and ill fortune as they move about outside the place of birth. On the twentieth day after birth a special growth ritual is said to "shape the character" of the infant until adult life begins. On the thirtieth day after birth the baby is taken to the households of the father's and mother's parents for a series of ritual acts. This formal visiting is intended to serve as a child's introduction to his kindred group members. At the father's parents' household one of three ritual growth acts is performed to "untie" the baby's growth and provide strength against disease and bad luck. Then the child is carried to the mother's parents' household where a ritual, "the small child goes to where it comes from," is said to formally affiliate it with the mother's kindred group. Then another growth ritual is recited to "untie" the child's luck.

Ceremonies at both houses are festive and last all day long. During rituals said for growth children have objects tied to their left wrist and right ankle as symbols of growth. Girls have small bracelets of shells or of silver to which a silver-cast bell is attached and boys have a silver bracelet, often with a small cast bell attached. Some parents also hold a party in their house the day after the ritual visits to the grandparents to celebrate the child having come to "one month of life." All the bilateral kindred members of the child are invited to the house to "meet" the baby. It is usual to also have a similar party at the child's first and fifth birthdays. Children are not generally given names until the fifth birthday and are not formally considered "persons" in their own right prior to their adolescence. It is believed that after five years the "character" begins to form and grow, and a child is supposed so show increasing responsibility for his acts, so that by 14 to 16 years he acts as an adult. After the first birthday no formal ritual is used for children, except those normally used for adults in life crises.

A newborn, of either sex, is termed *barAgAN,* or "red faced." Between six months and two years most children are given nicknames after particular sounds made or their ways of behaving. Names range from *lEmbegIt* ("holding on tightly"), *lEdtit* ("belly sticking out"), *gutEN* ("stinking"), *korEp* ("ears pulled close to the head") to *lAmpAs* ("slender faced-long legs"). Some persons are not named and go through their lives being called *barAgAN.*

Care and training of the Dusun child is set generally in the context of a series of values held by most village parents. These values tend to shape the ways children are treated and trained. Sensuron parents make many statements about their children and the tasks of child care and training. These statements can be summarized by organizing them into patterns of child training, which provide a means here for a brief discussion of transmission of custom from one Sensuron generation to the next. There are at least six patterns of enculturation that appear to give a distinctive nature to Dusun child training. These patterns are: (1) assumptions concerning the nature of children, (2) reward and punishment for behavior, (3) freedom from work responsibilities, (4) supernatural sanctions as controls for disruptive behavior, (5) judgment of a child as a "non-person," and (6) generational alteration of primary affective bonds.

These patterns of child training can be described briefly.

(1) *Nature of children:* Children are considered naturally noisy, inclined to illness, capable of theft, incurable wanderers, violent, quarrelsome, temperamental, destructive of property, wasteful, easily offended, quick to forget, and without sufficient character to blame for offenses against traditional law.

(2) *Reward and punishment:* Parents try to shape a child's generally contrary nature through use of specific techniques of rewarding and punishing behavior. Children are rewarded extensively with special allowances of favorite foods to encourage "good" behavior, and are praised lavishly with a variety of expressions such as "I am glad I have a child like this!" or, "Is that good child really mine?" More often Sensuron parents administer verbal or physical punishments to children for their disruptive behavior. Expressions such as *kAdAdA!* ("keep quiet!") and *nA! nA!* (do not!) are regularly heard in the village. At least five forms of overt physical punishment are recognized with some nine variations: (1) to hit with a stick; (2) to hit with rattan or a switch on the back, on the leg, and on the hand; (3) to twist an ear or cheek; (4) to snap with the thumb and middle finger on the ear or cheek; and (5) to slap with an open palm on the cheek or buttocks. All these forms of physical punishment are used regularly by parents. In a year of residence in Sensuron more than 175 separate instances were observed of a child being punished by one of these techniques. Ten-year-old children may respond to punishment by picking up sticks and striking back at parents. Not infrequently children respond to punishment through a display of hysterical behavior similar in form to hysterical acts exhibited by adults.

(3) *Freedom from work:* Until they are 11 or 12 years old children have

minimal responsibilities for household work tasks. Boys and girls of 6 to 12 years work regularly only at the task of going to the river to carry water; this task is a source of argument between parents and a child on nearly every occasion, and older children argue with younger brothers and sisters to force them to undertake this task for them. Most children under 12 years are not permitted to take part in gardening, or gathering tasks, and have only responsibilities for tending infants and brothers and sisters under 5 years of age. Infants usually are given to older sisters or brothers, and carried by them in cloth slings across the back. It is not unusual to see a 5-year-old or 6-year-old running in play with the head of an infant flopping from side to side on his back.

(4) *Supernatural sanctions:* Children are threatened constantly by parents with being eaten alive, carried off, injured, or damaged by disease givers, souls of the dead, or animals of the jungle. Lullabies reflect such threats, as in the verses sung to most village babies,

> Sleep, sleep, baby,
> There comes the *rAgun* (soul of the dead)
> He carries a big stick,
> He carries a big knife,
> Sleep, Sleep, baby,
> He comes to beat you!

or, as in this verse,

> Bounce, Bounce, baby
> There is a hawk,
> Flying, looking for prey!
> There is the hawk, looking for his prey!
> He searches for something to snatch up in his claws,
> Come here, hawk, and snatch up this baby!

(5) *Judgment of child as nonperson:* Children are judged not to be competent to participate in adult affairs, and thus are exempt from normal sanctions levied for offenses against traditional law. However, such exemption is basically a commitment by adults to the belief that children are not "persons" in the adult sense of the word. The practice of not providing personal names for children until their fifth year is part of the general belief by adults that children are not *tolun,* or "humans" until they exhibit expected adult knowledge and skills, and can conform to ideal standards of behavior. Thus a child not only does not have to live up to adult standards, he becomes aware very soon that it matters little if he were to do so.

(6) *Generational alternation of affective ties:* Children are taught to expect grandparents to be their protectors, benefactors, and champions with parents. Too, they learn that most of their personal character, attributes, and faults are ascribed to a grandparent with the same qualities of self rather than to a parent. And children learn to view many personal disputes as those directly inherited from a grandparent and still to be settled. Children also learn that disputes will arise because the other party to an argument has grandparents with

faults of character which lead to offenses against traditional law. A Sensuron child grows up in a world in which he is allied with his grandparent's generation, and expects that his own children will seek similar ties with his and his wife's parents. Village life is therefore cross-cut not only by factors of territory, wealth, and sex, but also by a generational alternation of basic affective ties.

Enculturation operates in such a manner as to be misleading to an observer from a Western European society. Infants and children are treated quite permissively in their relations with parents. There is little restriction on their behavior. Babies are breast fed on demand, toliet trained slowly and late, weaned gradually, and given great attention. In Western terms such ideally permissive child training could only lead to happy, independent, trusting and gentle adults. Dusun permissiveness, however, has none of the assumptions of the innate or natural value of the child common to the Western heritage and its premise, "each man has a dignity of worth of his own," nor do the patterns of child training function totally in a structure of enculturation in such a way to to produce gentle, trusting, and "happy" adults.

It is at puberty that a Dusun child finally comes to participation in the cultural system described in the preceding chapters. Before sexual maturity children are classed either as infants (*barAgAN*) or "children" (*INA tApe, INA sAntud;* "without a skirt," "without a loin cloth"). At the ages of 9 to 11 years for girls and boys, a covering is required over the genitals. From this age, until puberty "children" are considered "not yet adults," (*kAtAnAkun*), a condition that continues until full sexual maturity obviously is reached (*nAsukEd,* "he is grown," and *kesusunE,* "she has breasts"). Then, as the young man or woman exhibits skills, knowledge, and abilities of an adult, he or she becomes more and more a part of the regular social life of the village. Marriage and finally parenthood complete the age transitions in Sensuron enculturation to produce a man and a woman expected to follow traditional beliefs and ways.

World View

It is difficult to test formally the beliefs and expectations a people have about their life. This difficulty becomes compounded when it is necessary to cross cultural boundaries to secure data on such matters. Paper and pencil tests have an inherent defect in a society not accustomed to such ways of expression, and questions that seem perfectly sensible in a Western language become nonsensical in another language. With these hazards in mind and other qualifications that could also be discussed, it is still interesting to note the results of a test of dominant values and their variations, devised by F. Kluckhohn and F. L. Strodtbeck (1961) and revised by W. Caudill and H. A. Scarr (1962), when administered verbally to a sample of 70 Dusun adults and 40 children. The test comprises 18 items, grouped in 3 general headings of concerns with *time, relationships between men,* and *relations between man and nature.*

Dusun values, with reference to judgments of worthwhileness of behavior concerning relations between man and nature, appear dominated by a conviction that men must submit to most natural events, rather than seek means of control or prevention. Nature is believed a force beyond human power, especially in matters of fortune, life, health, and natural events. Men are believed to be able on occasion to work with nature in those specific conditions of daily life concerned with personal illness, agriculture, hunting, and property. In these instances the fortunes of men result from a continual striving to do proper things to maintain harmony with nature. This relationship is one-sided, for men know their efforts to maintain harmony with nature through submission and cooperation are not to be reciprocated generally, since natural forces have no concern for individuals.

A major variation of this value is held by a number of adults and some children. These persons expressed the belief that there is hope for a change in relations between men and nature to a condition where humans can come to dominate nature without antagonizing natural forces. This time is seen as part of a vague future condition.

Dusun are oriented predominantly to the past as a general guide for judgments regarding present or future behavior in child training, ceremonial practices, subsistence activities, and so on. Expressions concerning a philosophy of being are oriented to precedents of previous generations and established procedures. A major variation of this value placed on the past is an expectation that it is legitimate to expect a change in the future to a time when it will be possible to place emphasis on behavior standards, not because they have been used before, but because they are useful in solving problems of daily village life.

Dusun values concerning relations between men are dominated by the belief that ties which unite persons in the nuclear family households are primary in any situations involving questions of inheritance of land, personal property, and authority. However, behavior within the nuclear family unit is believed properly individualistic, with each adult responsible to himself in matters of behavior involving other family members. Any relations with persons outside the nuclear family household are believed best governed through customary forms that make men kin, for however short a time and for any task. A variation of this value is the belief expressed by some adults that *collateral* social relationships, established between equals, would some day be preferable to the *lineal* or authoritarian practice generally followed in social relations.

Most people of Sensuron are not aware generally of the contrasts between their expressed values and their regular ways of behavior. When such contrasts are noticed or brought to their attention, villagers tend to deal with them through the mechanisms used by people everywhere to defend the self from awareness of inconsistencies in belief and behavior; the Dusun are as capable and practiced at projection, rationalization, sublimation, and repression as any other humans. The content and style of these devices for defense of the self are uniquely Dusun, but, nonetheless, the people of Sensuron are quite capable and, occasionally, very skilled in use of such means to deal with their perception of differences between their professed beliefs and actual behavior. Within two hours of discussing with a male informant the social relations between Sensuron husbands and wives and learning that "men never beat their wives," I saw the informant strike his wife full in the face six times, knocking her through the open house door, across the porch and down the house steps. There he kicked her repeatedly while she lay curled up, screaming in rage and pain. When I asked the informant about the event, I learned he suspected his wife of adultery. I inquired concerning the difference between his statement of value that men do not beat their wives and the events of the past hour, and received the reply "I guess I did tell you that, did I not? Well, that is the way we are supposed to do things. This is a special case for she needs to be hit to make her learn."

A variety of inconsistencies of this type have been noted in this discussion of belief and behavior in Sensuron. These differences are recorded easily by an observer from another culture, for they are quickly perceived against the background of different beliefs and behavior.

Such differences can be frustrating in seeking to reduce descriptions of customary behavior to an orderly, systematic presentation, until it is learned that systems of customary behavior are not usually orderly and neatly arranged. Perhaps the greatest benefit an observer from another culture derives from his studies of local behavior is an awareness that other human customary behavior systems are also plagued by differences between what people say and the things they do, between the ideals they profess and the means used to achieve ends. Such contrasts and problems are obviously not the singular property of urbanized and industrial Western societies, nor an immutable force of the history of a particular civilization or region. However, an observer learns quickly also that in the society being studied there are individuals with an awareness of and concern about contrasts between professed belief and actual behavior.

Western society has often institutionalized this role in formal definitions such as "intellectual," "liberal," "scholar," "thinker," and so on. In Sensuron individuals keenly aware of contrasts between belief and behavior were scattered among both sexes, across adult age groups, and through the range of specialities of skills. Hence, not only the village headman and some ritual specialists, but a few "ordinary" village people were able to perceive and to discuss such contrasts, in several instances to speculate about the meaning of these differences, and on occasion to inquire in detail of the observer concerning existence of similar problems in his life. It is a mistake to assume that in an isolated community people are all alike, with little individual ability or capacity for learning, perceiving, and sometimes intellectually transcending the boundaries of their own time, place, and condition.

Culture Change

Changes have occurred in Dusun society for centuries. Life in Sensuron has changed since the founding of the community a century ago. More changes are occurring at present as the consequence of events taking place during a long period of British domination and exploitation, the Japanese army occupation of 1942–1945, and the formation of the state of Malaysia. Whether particular types of change in belief and behavior will continue or diminish in the next generation depends upon the agents of change, both in and outside of the village, and upon the structure of the Sensuron cultural behavior system as it now is comprised and functions.

Changes in some forms of dress, tools, weapons, and housing began soon after settlement of the village and were accelerated during the early period of British administration and as contacts with other cultural traditions became more frequent and on a first-hand basis. But the core of belief in religious behavior, omens, luck, sickness, death, social behavior, property, law, and subsistence remained generally unchanged until the decade prior to World War II, when British administrative officers began policies of active interference in these areas of local life through insisting that Anglo-Saxon codes of law, property, and some forms of subsistence be substituted for local customary behavior. At this time European Catholic missionaries also began active, first-hand efforts to change local belief and practices in religious behavior and conceptions of omens, luck, and fortune. Japanese troops were at first welcomed to the village as a means of reducing pressures for change that were building up on the part of the British government and European missions. In the later period of Japanese occupation, as interference in daily life became a feature of Japanese-Dusun contacts, the friendly relations turned to dislike, then hostility, as Japanese troops committed acts of murder, torture, rape, and plunder in the village. Reoccupation of the Tambunan area by British and Australian troops was accompanied by murders of many Japanese by village men. The re-establishment of civil government and return of the missionaries to the area again brought the same pressures for change that had been disliked and resisted before the war. In the time from 1946 to 1963 North Borneo civil administration operated under the direction of the British Colonial Office. In that 17-year period the people of Sensuron were deprived by a variety of techniques of political and personal freedoms and subjected to increasing pressures of change to European models of behavior and belief. For the most part these pressures were resisted, since both the British administrators and missionaries failed to comprehend the nature of the Dusun cultural behavior system and their own roles as agents of change.

The advent of Malaysia reduces the pressure for change to British models of behavior, but increases pressure for other changes, particularly for conformity to models of behavior derived from Malayan and overseas Chinese communities. The people of the village are now a self-governing unit, but with new ties to a district, state, and nation alien to their traditions and to their experience. Independence as citizens of Malaysia will bring health services and educational opportunities to the village not previously provided by the British. Most care in sickness and most of the formal schooling obtained by Dusun until 1961 was through the hard work, ingenuity, and self-sacrifice of a handful of Mill Hill Society missionaries,

Independence brings freedom of political action to shape a society to fit local circumstances. Whether this society will resemble the one described here must remain to be seen. A sympathetic observer can only hope that some of the perceptive and alert children of the village live and become educated to assume responsibility for direction and details of change in Dusun life at the local, state, and national level. Certainly, the opportunity for directed change is now available. Whether it is used depends upon the Dusun people and the events of the world and of Southeast Asia during the next decade.

Glossary

AFFINAL: Technical term used to describe marriage relationship between individuals, which links social groups. The *tengran* is formed in Dusun life through joining of bilateral kindreds by marriage relationship of members from different kindred groups. AFFINAL relatives are in-laws.

AMBILINEAL DESCENT GROUP: Technical term describing the *Dusun senAkAgun.*

ApAgEn: When a location or person is possessed of such an amount of magical, or *Asundu,* force that it is necessary to isolate the area or individual, the designation used is *ApAgEn.*

Asundu: A condition of magical sacredness derived from the force of creator beings.

ausEN: A force in the universe that punishes offenders of traditional behavior; see *seseAn.*

bAmbariEn: Female guardian spirit of the rice crop and storehouse.

bEbuleAn: Term applied to a female ritual specialist.

BILATERAL KINDRED: A social group based on recognition by members of their relationship to a particular individual, without regard to whether the relationship is through a male or female relative. A technical term for the Dusun *tengran.*

COLLATERAL SOCIAL RELATIONSHIPS: Social behavior in which personal power (see Chapter 7) generally exists for each individual in a corresponding measure. Opposite of LINEAL SOCIAL RELATIONSHIPS.

ENDOGAMY: Technical term for a rule of behavior which provides that members of a social group may marry only persons belonging to that group. In Dusun life members of the *senAkAgun* follow the rule of *endogamy.*

Erul genauE: A concept in which the "mind," or subconscious, wishes certain events to be true.

EXOGAMY: Technical term for a rule of behavior which provides that all members of a social group must marry persons not members of the group. In Dusun life members of a *tengran* follow the rule of *exogamy.*

gAgarAn: Act of being possessed by a familiar spirit being.

gEndIN: Ritual objects used by a female specialist that indicate possession by a familiar spirit in the act of divination of sickness or misfortune.

gemAt: A magically empowered object carried on the person to avoid bad luck.

HOABINHIAN: A term generally used to characterize an archeological culture of Southeast Asia in the period from 12,000 to 2,000 years ago and applied here to the classification of one stage of Borneo cultural history, with recognition that the term is being given special meaning.

HOMO PITHECANTHROPUS: An early form of human in Southeast and East Asia, and probably the earliest human population in Borneo.

INCEST: In Dusun life sexual intercourse, especially between a father and daughter, mother and son, brother and sister, and between a person and any opposite sexed member of his *tengran,* or bilateral kindred, is considered *sEmbAN,* or incest.

INDO-MALAYAN: A term used here to describe the appearance of native peoples in Borneo, Indonesia, and Malaya.

kAki kAki — kEdukEdu: Brother and sister, and first offspring of the creator beings, from whom all men and supernatural beings are supposed descended.

kAmbarANun: A cultivated marsh herb with a pungent rootstock odor used by the female ritual specialist in divination and curing acts.

kEmpetAs – sANerAn: Brother and sister offspring of *kAki kAki* and *kEdukEdu* who produced from their illicit intercourse all harmful spirits of the nonnatural world.

kerabau: Water buffalo

kInArINan: A term used to denote collectively all lesser creator beings, including *kAki kAki, kudukEdu, kudINkIN,* and *tINAleg.*

koboginan: A limited territorial grouping of nuclear family households.

kopeAn: A sign, or omen, of future events.

kudINkIN – tINAleg: Brother and sister offspring of *kAki kAki* and *kEdukEdu* who produced from their intercourse the Dusun people.

LEVIRATE: Technical term for a rule of behavior in which a widow may marry a brother of her deceased husband.

LINEAL SOCIAL RELATIONSHIPS: Social behavior in which personal power (see Chapter 7) is unequally distributed among and used by individuals as a consequence of factors of descent, age, sex, income, achieved status or any combination of such factors. Opposite of COLLATERAL SOCIAL RELATIONSHIPS.

MALAYO-POLYNESIAN: The name of the language stock spoken by natives of the Pacific area, except for some groups in Papuan New Guinea and the natives of Australia.

MAXIMAL RAMAGE-SEPT: Technical term used in describing the Dusun type of *ambilineal descent group,* where all members of a village usually belong to the same *senAkAgun,* or descent group.

mEgEndArAse: A magical personal power of the leader of a *senAkAgun* that is said to be used to frighten members into agreement.

mEgEndi: Term applied to the major ritual act of a female specialist in the supernatural.

mEnEmpEle: A ritual observance of return to the household of the final soul on the seventh night from burial of body.

megita: Mutual aid group formed by households, often those in a particular *koboginan,* which functions primarily in heavy work of planting, harvest, and house building.

MELANESIAN: A term used to describe the appearance of one group of Oceanic Negroid people inhabiting the islands to the east of New Guinea.

menemANEn: Male creator being.

MONSOON: From the Arab term "mausin," which denotes two wind phases each year, the wind prevailing in one being opposite to that prevailing in the other.

nApAN: A property payment made at marriage by the groom to the father of the bride.

narAnki: A ritual act of divination used by a female ritual specialist.

nauetAn: General term for property, which includes ten classes of "moveable" and two classes of "immoveable" property.

NEGRITO: A term applied to Asiatic and Oceanic pygmy peoples, and used here to refer to the general external characters of some native peoples living in Borneo, Philippines, and Malaya.

PADI RICE: Term used to describe rice grown in irrigated fields. Also called, "wet rice," or "irrigated rice."

parEndEnEn: Term applied to property left at burial to accompany the deceased to the afterworld.

pEkesusuon: The name of formal training in ritual conducted by a female specialist.

pENAluAn: The land of the dead.

pENININdApE: A magically endowed object carried on the person to enhance profit in trading of property.

rAgun: Human souls condemned by the creators to an eternity of wandering as cannibal spirits.

renit dE mENeAleg: Phrase used to describe the major ritual act of a male specialist in the supernatural.

rukeAn: Term applied to a male ritual specialist.

rusApAn: A magical antidote carried on the person, to be used for any attempts to poison or alter personal fortune.

sAgeAn: Practice of common ownership of particular types of property by members of a *senAkAgun,* or descent group.

sAgIt: A ritual fine paid to "cool" offense against the supernatural.

sEmbAN: The term used for incest, or sexual intercourse, between persons prohibited such acts by tradition, especially those belonging to the same *tengran,* or bilateral kindred. See *incest.*

senAkAgun: A descent group formed by recognition of village members that each is a descendent of a particular ancestor whose activities are told in legend and in whose name land is owned and special ritual is conducted.

seseAn: A force in the universe that punishes offenders of traditional behavior; see *ausEN.*

sumAsuai: A beneficial spirit with human attributes believed to assist men in times of crises.

sumInEndu: Female creator being.

SWIDDEN RICE: Technical term for rice grown without use of irrigation of fields. Also called "dry rice," "unirrigated rice," and "slash and burn agriculture."

tAmboreE: Supernatural beings felt responsible for giving disease to men.

tApun: A force in the universe that punishes individuals neglecting to honor agreements or refusing the hospitality of others, and thereby changing luck of the host.

tEnkosAn: Property inherited by an individual through membership in a bilateral kindred, or *tengran.*

tEtub: A token payment of property made by the groom to the father of the bride to accompany items paid as *nApAN* at marriage.

tengran: A social group comprised ideally in Dusun life of all living relatives from the great grandparents through the seventh cousins in the father's line of descent, and from great grandparents to third cousins in the mother's line of descent, with inclusion of all persons married to relatives in this group. Technically termed a *bilateral kindred.*

tINAleg – tAnduk: A symbol usually carved in bamboo that serves notice of a condition of *ApAgEn.*

tInAnAk – nAnAkAnAk: Objects used by a male ritual specialist in contacting the creator. Comparable to use of *kAmbarANun* root by female ritual specialist.

timbaN: A group of *koboginan* households considering themselves neighbors, and which functions in mutual aid, ceremonial, and political forms, including war.

USUFRUCT: Technical term applied to use of commonly owned property without impairing the substance of the goods. In Dusun life land, jars, gongs, and so on held as *sAgeAn,* or common property, of a *senAkAgun,* or descent group, can be used by members of the group without altering the common ownership rights of all members.

References Cited

CAUDILL, W. and H. A. SCARR, Japanese Value Orientations and Culture Change. *Ethnology,* 1:53–91, 1962.

HULSE, F. S., *The Human Species.* New York: Random House, 1963.

KLUCKHOHN, F., and F. L. STRODTBECK, *Variations in Value Orientations.* New York: Harper & Row, 1961.

LEACH, E. R., *Rethinking Anthropology.* London: London School of Economics Monographs on Social Anthropology, No. 22, Athlone Press, 1961.

Recommended Reading

EVANS, I. H. N., *Among Primitive Peoples in Borneo.* London: Seeley, Service and Company, 1922.

A useful description of particular areas of North Borneo, and of a variety of customary behavior forms of Dusun, Bajau, and Illanun peoples.

———, *The Religion of the Tempasuk Dusuns of North Borneo.* London: Cambridge University Press, 1953.

Broadly accurate descriptions of religious and other behavior forms of a coastal Dusun group.

FREEMAN, J. D., *Iban Agriculture.* London: Her Majesty's Stationery Office, Colonial Research Studies, No. 18, 1955.

A careful account of *Iban* customary behavior by a trained ethnographer. It is one of three reports of Sarawak peoples based on long-term residence in a native community.

GEDDES, W. R., *The Land Dayaks of Sarawak.* London: Her Majesty's Stationery Office, Colonial Research Studies, No. 14, 1954.

A competent description of Dayak customary behavior by a trained ethnographer.

HOSE, CHARLES, and WILLIAM MCDOUGALL, *The Pagan Tribes of Borneo.* London: Macmillan, 1912, 2 vols.

A generally informative account of a variety of forms of customary behavior among native peoples in Sarawak.

MORRIS, H. S., *Report on a Melanau Sago Producing Community in Sarawak.* London: Her Majesty's Stationery Office, Colonial Research Studies, No. 9, 1953.

One of three accounts of customary behavior among a Sarawak native people based on residence in a community by a trained observer.

ROTH, H. LING, *The Natives of Sarawak and North Borneo.* London: Truslove and Hanson, 1896, 2 vols.

An editing and supplementing by Roth of the notes of Hugh Low, made after Low's death in 1887. Notes in these volumes are valuable for comparative studies.

RUTTER, OWEN, *The Pagans of North Borneo.* London: Hutchinson, 1929.

A description of some Dusun customary behavior forms.

WILLIAMS, THOMAS RHYS, A Survey of Native Peoples of North Borneo. *Sociologus,* 10:170–74, 1960.

A discussion of ethnic groups in North Borneo.

———, A Tambunan Dusun Origin Myth. *Journal of American Folklore,* 74:68–78, 1961.

The translated text of a folktale of Dusun origin and creation.

———, Ethnohistorical Relationships and Patterns of Customary Behavior Among North Borneo Native Peoples. *Sociologus,* 11:51–63, 1961.
A discussion of some major patterns of customary behavior in North Borneo.
———, Form, Function and Culture History of a Borneo Musical Instrument. *Oceania,* 32:178–185, 1962.
An account of the manufacture, use, and possible cultural historical origins of a Borneo musical instrument.
———,Tambunan Dusun Social Structure, *Sociologus,* 12:141–157, 1962.
A description and analysis in anthropological terms of Dusun social structure.
———, Archaeological Research in North Borneo. *Asian Perspectives: The Bulletin of the Far-Eastern Prehistory Association,* 6:230–231, 1962.
A description of a variety of North Borneo archaeological sites likely to be productive of cultural historical data.
———, The Form and Functions of Tambunan Dusun Riddles. *Journal of American Folklore,* 76:95–110; 141–181, 1963.
A presentation and discussion of the social functions of riddles in Dusun life.
———, The Form of a North Borneo Nativistic Behavior. *American Anthropologist,* 65:543–551, 1963.
A description of some reactions of *Murut* peoples to contacts with Europeans.
———, Cultural Structuring of Tactile Experiences in a Borneo Society. *American Anthropologist,* in press, 1965.
An account of the ways the sense of touch is shaped and elaborated in Dusun life.

Readings on Native Peoples of Southeast Asia

Each reference contains other citations to readings on native peoples of a particular area.

General

COLE, FAY-COOPER, *The Peoples of Malaysia.* New York: Van Nostrand, 1945.
LEBAR, FRANK M., GERALD C. HICKEY, and JOHN K. MUSGRAVE, *Ethnic Groups of Mainland Southeast Asia.* New Haven, Conn.: Human Relations Area Files, 1964.

Philippines

CONKLIN, H. C., *Hanunóo Agriculture in the Philippines.* Rome: Food and Agriculture Organization of the United Nations, Forestry Paper No. 2, 1957.

Malaya

EVANS, I. H. N., *Negritos of Malaya.* London: Cambridge University Press, 1937.

Burma

LEHMAN, F. K. *The Structure of Chin Society. A Tribal People of Burma Adapted to a Non-Western Civilization.* Urbana, Ill.: University of Illinois Studies in Anthropology, No. 3, 1963.

Laos

IZIKOWITZ, KARL GUSTAV, *Lamet: Hill Peasants in French Indochina.* Göteborg, Sweden: Etnologiska Studier, No. 17, Göteborg Museet, 1951.

Vietnam

MAITRE, HENRI, *Les Jungles Moi.* Paris: Larose, 1912.

Thailand

YOUNG, GORDON, *The Hill Tribes of North Thailand.* Bangkok: The Siam Society, Monograph No. 1, 1961.

East Pakistan

BESSAIGNET, PRESSE, *Tribesmen of the Chittagong Hill Tracts.* Dacca: Asiatic Society of Pakistan, Publication No. 1, 1958.

East India—Assam

BURLING, ROBBINS, *Rengsanggri: Family and Kinship in a Garo Village.* Philadelphia: University of Pennsylvania Press, 1963.

India

VYDYARTHI, L. P., *The Maler: Nature—Man—Spirit Complex in a Hill Tribe of Bihar.* Calcutta: Bookland Private Ltd., 1962.

Indonesia

CHABOT, H. TH., *Kinship, Status and Sex in South Celebes.* New Haven, Conn.: Translation in Human Relations Area Files, on Macassar (File OG-6). Groningen-Jakarta: J. B. Wolters, 1950.

DUBOIS, CORA, *The People of Alor.* Minneapolis: University of Minnesota Press, 1944.

Formosa

HWEI-LIN, WEI, Patri-Lineage and Bilateral Corporate Group of the Yami. *The Bulletin of the Institute of Ethnology, Academia Sinica* 7:1–41, 1959.

CASE STUDIES IN CULTURAL ANTHROPOLOGY

GENERAL EDITORS—George and Louise Spindler

BEING A PALAUAN *H. G. Barnett*

GOPALPUR: A SOUTH INDIAN VILLAGE *Alan R. Beals*

BUNYORO: AN AFRICAN KINGDOM *John Beattie*

THE TWO WORLDS OF THE WASHO *James F. Downs*

HANO: A TEWA INDIAN COMMUNITY IN ARIZONA *Edward P. Dozier*

VASILIKA: A VILLAGE IN MODERN GREECE *Ernestine Friedl*

THE TIWI OF NORTH AUSTRALIA *C. W. M. Hart and Arnold R. Pilling*

THE MAGARS OF BANYAN HILL *John T. Hitchcock*

THE CHEYENNES: INDIANS OF THE GREAT PLAINS *E. Adamson Hoebel*

A GUADALCANAL SOCIETY: THE KAOKA SPEAKERS *Ian Hogbin*

THE SWAZI: A SOUTH AFRICAN KINGDOM *Hilda Kuper*

ULITHI: A MICRONESIAN DESIGN FOR LIVING *William A. Lessa*

TEPOZTLÁN: VILLAGE IN MEXICO *Oscar Lewis*

THE MEXICAN-AMERICANS OF SOUTH TEXAS *William Madsen*

THE LUGBARA OF UGANDA *John Middleton*

KNOWING THE GURURUMBA *Philip L. Newman*

CHANGING JAPAN *Edward Norbeck*

LIFE IN A TURKISH VILLAGE *Joe E. Pierce*

THE KAPAUKU PAPUANS OF WEST NEW GUINEA *Leonard Pospisil*

THE IGBO OF SOUTHEAST NIGERIA *Victor C. Uchendu*

THE DUSUN: A NORTH BORNEO SOCIETY *Thomas Rhys Williams*

HOLT, RINEHART AND WINSTON, INC.

383 Madison Ave., New York, N. Y., 10017